The Practice of Godliness

The Practice of Godliness

by

DR. ABRAHAM KUYPER

Author of
"To Be Near Unto God,"
"The Holy Spirit," etc.

Translated and Edited by
Marian M. Schoolland

WM. B. EERDMANS PUBLISHING COMPANY
Grand Rapids   1948   Michigan

THE PRACTICE OF GODLINESS
by Dr. Abraham Kuyper

Copyright, 1948, *by*
Wm. B. Eerdmans Publishing Company
All rights in this book are reserved. No part may be reproduced in any manner without permission in writing from the publisher, except brief quotations used in connection with a review in a magazine or newspaper.

Set up and printed, January, 1948

PRINTED IN THE UNITED STATES OF AMERICA

Publisher's Preface

Dr. Abraham Kuyper, the great Dutch religious and political leader of the turn of the century, was a many-sided genius. He was known throughout the world as a distinguished preacher, editor, and author of many books. For decades he was the leader of the Christian political party in The Netherlands and for a time served as the country's Prime Minister. He was the founder of the Free University of Amsterdam, and his almost superhuman energy evidenced itself in almost every field of human endeavor.

Probably the most lasting monument to his vast influence is the great fund of devotional literature which he left in many volumes — writings which, like his *To Be Near Unto God*, rank with the devotional classics such as Thomas a Kempis' *Imitation of Christ*. The heritage which Dr. Kuyper left is for the edification of sincere Christians of every creed and group. His lofty ideals and Isaiah-like utterances are treasures to be preserved and cherished by many generations.

As Dr. John Hendrik de Vries, who has translated many of Dr. Kuyper's works, says: "The more one acquaints himself with the vast scope of the varied labors of this man, the more deeply one becomes impressed with the significance of the devotional, mystical output of his pen. Profound theological learning, great statesmanship, extraordinary intellectual acumen along any line is not thought as a rule to be compatible with childlike simplicity of faith, mystical insight and sweetness of soul. But in the words of a reviewer, 'Kuyper's meditations disprove the idea that a profound theologian cannot be a warm-hearted Christian.'"

Personally, I think that *The Practice of Godliness* is one of Dr. Kuyper's finest works. It is filled with insight into the character of the mystical union of Christ and the believer. For a long time I had hoped to find a translator to bring this devotional gem to the American public in proper fashion. Now, with Miss Marian Schoolland's excellent rendition ready, I am very grateful and happy to issue this English edition of *The Practice of Godliness,* in the hope that it may prove a comfort and help to many Christians and Christ-seekers.

WM. B. EERDMANS

Contents

Part I — THE CHRISTIAN WARFARE

I.	Our Troubled Lives	11
II.	Man Versus Satan	19
III.	Man Versus Nature	27
IV.	Man Versus Man	36
V.	The Church of Jesus Christ	47

Part II — CHRISTIAN PATIENCE

I.	Patience a Rarity	65
II.	We Glory in Strength	67
III.	For Love of God	70
IV.	A Strength of the Spirit	74
V.	Meekness	78
VI.	The Man of Sorrows	82
VII.	Maranatha	86
VIII.	Cross Bearing	90

Part III — HUMILITY BEFORE GOD

I.	God's Word Our Guide	97
II.	Biblical Fasting	101
III.	Godliness	106
IV.	Not by Bread Alone	110
V.	Seek Ye First	115
VI.	In the Home	119

PART I

THE CHRISTIAN WARFARE

> ". . . War the good warfare, holding faith and a good conscience. . . ."
>
> I Timothy 1:18, 19.

OUR TROUBLED LIVES

I

Our Troubled Lives

Working the Work of the Lord

ZERUBBABEL was beset with troubles when the angel brought him the Word of the Lord through the prophet: "Not by might, not by power, but by my Spirit, saith the Lord of hosts" (Zechariah 4:6).

How often we have heard those words applied to problems of today, as if they were a warning against human effort in Kingdom work! But they were not that. Indeed not—for the Lord encouraged Zerubbabel in the work of his hands. The angel says, "The hands of Zerubbabel have laid the foundation of this house, and his hands shall also finish it." The Spirit of the Lord, using the hands of Zerubbabel, would accomplish the work, though physical might and power to match that of the enemy was lacking in the little band of zealous workers.

There are Christians who maintain that the godly life is a life of quiet submission, of patient waiting—waiting upon the Lord, till He perform His own work. "For the battle is the Lord's" and "Jehovah shall fight for you," they say.

In Old Testament times it did occur that Jehovah bade His people stand aside and wait. When Israel was before the Red Sea, panic-stricken at the sound of Pharaoh's armed horseman coming after them, the Lord gave command,

"Do not fight! I will fight for you!" And they stood still, while the waves of the sea awaited His Word of power.

Why was Israel spared a bloody battle and permitted to walk safely and comfortably through the Red Sea? Because the Lord was about to perform a miracle at which all the nations would stand amazed, making the bottom of the Sea a pathway for Israel and a grave for Pharaoh and all his host. And, in order that His power and greatness might shine forth with greater glory, the miracle must be wholly free from human mediation.

God works by one of two methods—through man or without man, mediately or immediately.

When He chooses to work immediately, He commands man to stand aside, to be still and wait, to keep hands off.

But the era of such miraculous intervention is past. Wonders such as of old God does not choose to perform now, though at the return of Jesus upon the clouds He will again thus gloriously manifest His power. In the meantime, He is working mediately, through us. And it is ours to be up and doing; ours to work the work of the Lord; ours to labor in the Name of the Lord, amid troubles that beset us on every hand.

Let us be warned, however, that mere human effort, labor not inspired by the One in whose hand are all things, is vain and abominable. A man may *think* that he labors in the Name of the Lord, yet be busy in his own strength and for himself.

It is important that we *know*.

Whence Our Troubles Come

The Christian life is not an easy life. We, like Zerubbabel, are beset by enemies.

OUR TROUBLED LIVES

In general the powers that constantly oppose and threaten us are three: nature, man, and fallen angels. Our troubles and miseries always come from one or the other of these three. And now the question to be considered is this: What attitude would God have us take toward these three and the troubles they bring?

First let us consider what is involved.

Nature is arrayed against us in practically all of its activities. Instead of living in Paradise, we are in a restless world where there is little peace or harmony. Immediately after the fall, God drove man out of Paradise and told him that the world would henceforth be in enmity against him. It would bring forth thorns and thistles; where it once grew fruit in abundance for the picking, it would now yield the best only if man labored hard. Woman must bear children in pain. And at last the earth would triumphantly reclaim man—the most beautiful creature of God's making must return to dust.

Throughout history men have found this pronouncement of God true, and it is true today.

What a world it is! Storms at sea have swallowed up untold numbers of victims. From the depths of earth ominous rumblings arise, and the earth trembles under volcanic pressure. Cloudburst, hail, frost, heat, flood and fire and wind—they all bring ruin and death.

Nature further vents its fury against man in a thousand plagues aimed at his very life. Pestilence creeps out of stagnant swamp and dense jungle. Invisible microbes and viruses enter our very blood and bones. Disease rages among the cattle from which we obtain food. We must constantly be watchful against hordes of insects. Little creatures such as the field mouse decimate our crops, and strong wild beasts

THE PRACTICE OF GODLINESS

of the forest prey upon human beings. Because of sin nature has been so disrupted that it makes a dreadful picture.

Nature also resists the birth of every child, so that women everywhere moan in travail. And men by the millions are bowed under the burden of toil for daily food.

Then there is the inevitable final triumph of nature over every human being, for his body shall decay and the earth shall reclaim its own.

Beautiful nature! But how terrible is the destructive power which it wields against man!

Man's struggle with man is of a different kind. Among men there is love and hatred, and both bring suffering. Yes, love brings joy and beauty and comfort. But it also brings sorrow. For because of love we share the sorrow of others and our sorrow also becomes theirs. Ask a mother if she does not suffer just because she loves her child so dearly!

At the root of man's enmity to man, however, lies hatred. Not that we need live in mortal fear lest someone knock us down, rob us, or kill us, out of pure hatred. That seldom happens. The situation is much more complicated. It is this: We cannot each walk our little path alone. We must have contact with other people—in social, civil, business or other activities. And then two possibilities are usually present—either we step back and let the other fellow have top place, or we keep the other fellow down and capture the booty ourselves. The result is jealousy, envy, pride, disobedience, suspicion, deceit, falsehood—a host of evils that are poison in the human heart. To a man of noble character they give grief and pain. In the man of little soul they breed hatred and revenge.

OUR TROUBLED LIVES

Then there is the worst and deadliest of man's enemies, the devil—the worst because he has an ally within the heart of each one of us.

Years may slip by before we notice what is going on, that we are being gradually dragged down to hell. While we are blissfully unaware, evil grows and flourishes in our hearts. Until Christ comes to claim us. Then, when the evil must out, the struggle begins. What a struggle it is! Temptation luring us with a terrible power. Satan holding on fiercely to his prey. There are times when we cry out in agony.

Those who live deeply experience it thus.

Many, very many, live superficially and never experience much of a struggle. They protest that such a view of life is too dismal and morbid.

There are some who try to whistle away their troubles, and some who hide an embittered heart behind laughing lips.

But that does not change facts. If you would know the true character of life, ask the man who seeks to know the truth, and who has matured in the experiences of life. He will tell you that which men of long ago also affirmed: Life is at best a struggle. Our years may number seventy, or if we are very strong eighty, but they are filled with labor and sorrow.

Finally—and this brings us face to face with the awful seriousness of life—trouble and sorrow has come upon us *from God*. He has willed it. He has deemed it necessary.

Therein we see God's righteousness, and also His Providence. For all God's attributes are but the vari-colored rays emanating from the Divine Being. Thus His Providence and the vindication of His righteousness go hand in hand.

THE PRACTICE OF GODLINESS

Man sinned. And a sinner could not remain in Paradise. He did not belong there.

A ruined man is at home in a ruined world.

Since man took a stand of enmity against God, it is right that enmity should be arrayed against him. We *must* have enemies, even deadly enemies.

And the Lord God loosed against man three enemies: nature, man, and the demons.

Thus we are daily the targets of evil forces that plot against our welfare and against our very lives. The Lord has willed it so. Enemies are before us and behind us, visible and invisible, waylaying, tripping, instigating, oppressing, day and night.

Whether the arrow is in the form of lightning from the sky, or an angry denunciation by a friend, or an evil suggestion within the heart whispered by Satan, it is always intended for the ruin of our souls. We are the targets. The evil may come in many attractive forms, but it is aimed at your soul's life. Evil will beset you and hound you, and would surely choke you did you not escape to the City of Refuge.

Living by Principle

We Christians, members of the Body of Christ, live our mundane lives from day to day. We speak, we plan, we decide, we act. But it is well to pause for a moment and ask the question: On what ground do we make our decisions and plan our actions? Why do we choose to do thus and so, rather than otherwise? What guides us in our planning and doing?

The actual conditions today, as we look about for an answer to that question, are enough to make one weep. For we find that leaders as well as laymen (with a few precious

OUR TROUBLED LIVES

exceptions) have completely forgotten that there is such a thing as principle, that there is a rule by which to measure our everyday activities. Each does "as it seems good in his own eyes."

What we choose to do or not do is no longer, it seems, a matter of must—a must founded upon the eternal principles of God's Word and Will. What we do is a matter of our own choosing.

For one will say, "This is the way he does it, and that looks good to me." At another time he may say, "I made good by that course of action; I shall use the same method again." Or, "This is what he wants done, and it is my business to please him." Some say, "Oh, I just happened to feel like doing that!" Or, "It *works* best that way!"

We are sorely in need of a reminder that there is only one guiding principle for all Christian activity, for every choice and action in the life of a Christian. That guiding principle asks: What is the will of God concerning this?

Now in regard to the subject at hand. We are beset by three evil forces—the devil, sinners, and nature's destructions; or let us say—by fallen angels, fallen man, and fallen nature: And the question arises: What would God have us do about it? Would He have us submit without struggle or self-defence to the powers that threaten us? Or does He require that we shall defend ourselves?

Note that the question is not: *May* we defend ourselves?

That would lead to a weak and spineless Christianity, springing from some such philosophy as this: God is high above; we here below, seeking to satisfy our own desires, must try not to incur His displeasure; but for the most He will in loving-kindness overlook our human frailties and our errors.

THE PRACTICE OF GODLINESS

No, my dear reader, our God is not that kind of God.

He is THE LORD OF HOSTS. His are the hosts of heaven. And with His creatures upon earth He does whatsoever He wills.

The Lord of lords, the Almighty, has a *will*. A will that applies in every case, and to every person. How can we possibly conceive of a God who waits to see what shall happen?

Therefore the reasoning in regard to our present problem is not: What will God *let* us do? Will He permit us to protect ourselves if we so wish?

Such would be a dishonor to His Name.

Such a God would not be a God clothed in majesty.

No! The question must be put thus: The God who, because of our sins, loosed against us the three destructive powers, did He intend that we should resist them and defend ourselves? Or did He intend that we should be overwhelmed by these evils?

He who would live the Godly life seeks to know the *will* of God exactly. He asks no more and no less.

That applies in this matter also. It must.

And what that will of God may be we cannot conclude from our own opinions, or from our own whims and wishes. The question must be answered from the Lord's own revelation. Has He revealed His will on this question? If so, what is it? How must we act overagainst the three inimical powers arrayed against us—the devil, sinners, and natural disasters? The Thorns and Thistles, the Cains, and the Old Serpent?

The answer is not easy. It is complicated, many sided.

Let us begin where we can see our way most clearly and easily, with the spiritual struggle Satan brings upon us.

MAN VERSUS SATAN

II.

Man Versus Satan

Who Is Satan?

GOD created Satan. He made Satan a superior and splendid creature. We may safely say that Satan has qualities which place him in a supreme position among all God's creatures. Sincere Christians have even called him the rival of the Lord Jesus Christ. And not without reason. Consider how Scripture contrasts him with the Christ, as it were putting them on one level. Satan is the ruler of the hosts of evil, Christ is Head of the armies of the Lord. Scripture pictures for us two spirit kingdoms, each with its leader, and in opposition to each other. For neither among the good angels nor among men is there any leader over against Christ. Only Satan, head of the hosts of evil spirits, has that appalling position of power.

Further, let us remember that Christ has His great authority and power only as "God revealed in the flesh." But Satan, for all his astounding power, is a mere creature! One cannot help wondering what he might have become, had he not rebelled, had he remained in his angelic state! Even now, though fallen away from God through mutiny, he inspires us with awe; to what grandeur might he not have risen if, instead of falling *away* from God, he had fallen down before Him in eternal worship and devotion?

THE PRACTICE OF GODLINESS

But such an one, terrible in power and inspired with unquenchable hatred against Jesus Christ and His people, is our adversary.

We give too little thought to that power of Satan. We do not realize — not by far do we realize — how great is the power of horrible unholiness which is ever pressing upon us, ever ready to attack, bent upon destroying us; nor do we realize how wonderful is the fullness of grace and power that is at work every moment, mercifully shielding our poor souls and the souls of our children against the sinister and fearful foe.

As you grow in realization of the terrifying power of Satan, you will cling the closer to God, call upon Him the more fervently, and thank Him with more ardent love for the deliverance wrought through Jesus Christ, your Saviour.

Satan is well aware of the fact that nothing interferes with his purpose more than man's recognition of him. Therefore he seeks, with his usual cunning and craft, to make men believe that he does not exist. For if there is no Satan, it is folly to be afraid of him. Then, too, since we do not need a protection against an evil being who is mere figment of man's imagination, if there is no Satan we have no need of God and **His Christ.**

Satan has no difficulty finding helpers who gladly teach and preach such false peace. And then he is in his element, he has free play. When it is considered intelligent and refined to scoff at belief in a Satan, then he reaps his richest harvest of corrupted human hearts, of unhappy opinion and insolently leads even nations astray. Those are tragic days for mankind.

MAN VERSUS SATAN

But the outlook for the nation, the home, and the individual becomes more hopeful when once again men are keenly aware of Satan's activity, when men once again take him into account in daily life.

For when we realize that Satan is busy and at his tricks, then we are on our guard; then we seek refuge in Him who has crushed Satan's head; then we close our hearts to the stealthy, murderous enemy.

Ponder the situation for a moment. Try to grasp the terrible import. Here is a creature with exceptional talents, with gifts and capacities immeasurably greater than those of any human being. Though fallen, he yet has the nature of an angel and therefore is able to influence men in a manner far beyond our understanding; and he is surrounded by an unnumbered host of other fallen angels who zealously and fanatically aid him in all his hateful efforts to destroy men. Truly, is it not enough to make one tremble? It is a wonder that a child of God, comprehending something of the horrible danger, welcomes the question: What is your only comfort in life and in death? And rejoices in the answer: My only comfort is this that I am not my own but belong to the Lord Jesus Christ, *who has rescued me from all the power of the devil* and so preserves me that without the will of my heavenly Father not a hair can fall from my head.

We shall not now discuss further the extent of Satan's power over mankind. In the days of witchcraft that power was no doubt exaggerated, or at least there were false imputations. But it is equally true that in our day his power is greatly underestimated. According to the Word of God, we know that Satan is implicated in suffering such as Job endured, in sorcery, in certain types of insanity, in the deceiv-

THE PRACTICE OF GODLINESS

ing of the nations, in temptations of individuals, in acts of violence and enmity against the church of Christ.

* * *

Further investigation of Scripture brings us to another question regarding the power of Satan: Can it be that the coming of Jesus to earth has disarmed Satan? Was Calvary his downfall? Did he there lose the great power which he had in olden times?

Many believe that to be so. For God said to the Satan in Paradise, "The seed of the woman shall bruise thy head." And the apostle John declares that Christ came "that He might destroy the works of the devil." Therefore, they argue, Satan is through. His power was crushed at Calvary. The roaring lion has been led captive and is now helpless.

But on the basis of God's Word that idea must be declared false. True indeed, we are told that Christ crushed Satan and conquered the might of his kingdom on Calvary—in principle. But the Scriptures just as emphatically declare that Satan will not be thrown into the pool of fire until the end time, and also that he will strive yet more fiercely and bitterly against Christ and His people. Jesus taught us to pray, "Deliver us from the evil one." The apostles warned their early converts again and again to beware of evil powers of the air, of the prince of the realm of darkness; and throughout the nineteen centuries of the Christian era devout children of God have struggled with the evil one. Think of Luther!

No. Today, this very day, we are by no means free from Satan's activity. We are still subject to his attacks and deceivings; he injects his poisonous profanities even into our very prayers.

MAN VERSUS SATAN

Resisting Satan

Must we be passive when Satan attacks and torments us? Or must we resist him and contend with him? Does the Bible teach us to struggle? Or to submit humbly to the abuses of Satan?

You may say, "That question is almost blasphemous!"

And yet I assure you that there are those for whom the question is not strange, and who answer that we must be passive because Satan's attacks are God's punishment upon us.

On the other hand, for those who believe in the free will of God's creatures, the question has no meaning. They think of Satan as acting wholly on his own, outside of God's control. To them God is not the Supreme One, who has all things in His Hand. They make God dependent, and thus rob Him of His Godhead. Therefore they would not think of asking such a question. They are entirely outside this discussion.

But all who believe in the absolute sovereignty of God confess with us that Satan, too, is a creature; and therefore he, too, is one of God's subjects and can do nothing apart from the will of God. His temptations and attacks are always under God's control. Without the will of our Father in heaven, Satan cannot harm a hair of our head. *All* is under God's domain. Satan has no right over us.

The Lord's prayer, "Lead us not into temptation but deliver us from the evil one," implies clearly that, though God does not tempt us, nevertheless the temptations which come upon us are not outside the sphere of Divine provi-

dence; and it further implies that God is able to shield His children against the evil one and to keep them safe through the gravest danger.

If then this is our sincere confession, that the temptations of Satan are as much a part of Divine providence as are sickness and trouble and war, then obviously one question holds for all, whether it be pestilence or the enmity of fellow-men or the wiles of Satan that distress us: If God has brought this illness, or this trouble, or this satanic temptation upon me, is it His will that I shall nevertheless resist it? Or ought I to submit to it, humbly drinking the bitter cup to its dregs without protest?

Those who teach passivity in suffering even over against Satan's attacks have reasoned the matter out. They ask "Does not the Bible teach that God has given Satan the liberty to molest us?" And when we answer affirmatively they ask, "And does it not follow, then, that we may not resist? For surely, God lets such troubles come because they must come!" Thus they conclude by their own *reasoning* that resistance to Satan cannot be in accordance with the will of God.

We protest most solemnly against such reasoning. What do we know of God's purposes and intentions? Nothing except what He is pleased to tell us in His Word.

And to this question the Scripture gives clear and decisive answer, in specific pronouncements.

Note the three-fold teaching of the Bible: The *fact* that God does permit Satan to molest us; the *revelation* that nevertheless God wills that we resist Satan; and some *suggestions* which help clear the apparent contradiction. We shall discuss each of these briefly.

MAN VERSUS SATAN

The *fact,* namely that Satan can do nothing against us without or apart from the will of God. This is clearly evident from the story of Job. And it is further clear from the general teaching throughout Scripture that the Lord is God Almighty, Ruler over *all His creatures.*

The *revelation,* namely that we should nevertheless resist Satan and all his evil host with all our might: "Neither give place to the devil" (Eph. 4:27). "Put on the whole armor of God, that ye may be able *to stand against* the wiles of the devil. For our *wrestling* is not against flesh and blood, but against the principalities, against the powers, against the world-rulers of this darkness, against the spiritual hosts of wickedness in heavenly places. Wherefore *take up the whole armor of God,* that ye may be able to *withstand* in the evil day, and, having done all, to stand" (Eph. 6:11-13). *"Resist the devil and he will flee from you"* (James 4:7). ". . . Your adversary the devil, as a roaring lion, walketh about seeking whom he may devour; *whom resist* . . ." (I Peter 5:8, 9).

And finally some *suggestions* to clear up the apparent contradiction that God, having loosed Satan to be our adversary, yet requires that we resist him with all our might. In the first place, God lets Satan put us through the fire of trial that our faith may be manifested as valuable gold, pure and genuine, to His glory; think of Job. Secondly, by means of such provocation God reveals unto us our own spiritual weakness. In the third place, our Lord uses Satan as a shepherd uses his dog to drive the sheep to the shepherd. And fourthly, God must triumph over Satan not by hindering his activities, but by first letting him put forth all his might and then overthrowing him with His Divine Supremacy.

THE PRACTICE OF GODLINESS

Satan's driving desire is to lay hold upon us and drag us away from Jesus. And because our hearts are so prone to evil, he would most certainly succeed if Jesus did not pray for us. It is a horrible thought—to be sifted by Satan as wheat is sifted! But there is also the wonderfully comforting assurance, "No man can pluck them out of my hand!"

Alongside that assurance from the lips of our precious Saviour stands the command, "Resist the devil!"

III

Man Versus Nature

The Enmity of Nature

WE have concluded that resistance to the onslaughts of Satan is not merely permissible. It is commanded.

We will now take up the next question, a slightly more complicated one: What should our attitude be toward the troubles which come upon us from natural sources—the sicknesses, the suffering, the destruction, the common daily reverses as well as the great and sudden calamities? Should we meekly accept them and surrender to their power over us? Or is it God's will that we resist them in His Name, and defend ourselves against them?

First of all let us once again confess, humbly and devoutly, that "nothing can befall us by chance, but by the direction of our most gracious and heavenly Father"—a confession which includes the everyday occurrences as well as the extraordinary, a confession which asserts positively and unquestionably that everything is in God's hand and that without His will the powers of nature cannot so much as stir.

God is God. Let us ever *keep* Him God in our thoughts and considerations. All the devotion and all the true piety of our confession is based upon the exalted concept that God is *absolutely* God. We *dare* to believe that. He has counted us worthy to uphold that supreme teaching of His Word.

THE PRACTICE OF GODLINESS

Clearly, that confession negates all possibility of separating daily common hardships from great calamities, as if the first came upon us by chance and only the latter were "providential" or God-sent.

Whatever threat or danger or destruction may come upon us from nature, we must accept it as coming from God, directed toward us and inflicted upon us by Him. There cannot be any exception, not even the smallest.

Recall once more what happened immediately after the Fall.

The Lord told Adam and Eve plainly that nature would from then on be a fearful power, an enemy, even an enemy unto death.

When God made man, He crowned him lord of creation, ruler of all nature. "Replenish the earth, and subdue it!" With that injunction man was given authority to discover earth's hidden riches and use them and control them. He was given dominion over all.

But how tragically different that becomes after the Fall! Earth is now commanded to bring forth thorns and thistles for man, to refuse him its fruits, to make man wrestle for his daily bread, and finally, when man is worn and weary of the struggle, to conquer him and return him to dust. Nature henceforth the conqueror! All of that is implied in God's word to Adam: "Cursed is the ground for thy sake; in toil shalt thou eat of it all the days of thy life; thorns also and thistles shall it bring forth to thee; and thou shalt eat the herb of the field; in the sweat of thy face shalt thou eat bread, till thou return unto the ground; for out of it wast thou taken; for dust thou art and unto dust shalt thou return." And there is an added poignancy in His word to the woman,

MAN VERSUS NATURE

"I will greatly multiply thy pain and thy conception; in pain thou shalt bring forth children; and thy desire shall be to thy husband, and he shall rule over thee."

* * *

There are two truths implied in this curse upon the earth for man's sake. The first is this, that neither man nor woman can escape suffering. It is unavoidable. Any attempt to build about ourselves an imaginary paradise from which all sorrow has been charmed away is self-deception, and is also contrary to the will of God. For He has ordained that man shall suffer.

And the second is equally evident—man must not merely resign himself to his fate. He is rather called upon to be the more active, to struggle valiantly against the powers that would destroy him.

Man might be inclined to think: "Since I have to die some day and return to dust, it may as well be now. Why should I struggle with these thorns and thistles? Why should I sow and labor for a harvest? I shall simply let myself starve to death." But God commands him to work, to labor, to battle with nature, to wrest from the earth the food it no longer gives willingly to nurture his life and prolong it. And the woman may not say, "I will escape the sorrow and pain; I will not bear children!" For though nature will resist the coming of new life, making childbirth difficult and painful, woman is called to wrest that new life from nature, be it with pain and agony.

The man and woman who bravely and courageously take up the struggle against the earth which would withhold its life-giving food and against the womb which would withhold the new life stirring within it, they are comforted with the

THE PRACTICE OF GODLINESS

assurance of God's blessing. But the lazy man who refuses to labor, and the weakling woman who refuses to accept her lot of suffering, forfeit that blessing.

The struggle against nature, then, is not a struggle to escape pain and suffering or to banish suffering from one's life. But it is a struggle in holy faith, knowing that we *cannot* escape suffering, that it *must* be our lot, and also knowing that through suffering the glory of God will shine more resplendently in the lives of men.

Resisting Nature's Enmity

There is an almost unquenchable longing in man's being to avoid pain; we instinctively yearn to banish suffering from the earth, if possible.

But that tendency of the human heart is sinful. It is as if man thought himself worthy of all good, as if sorrow and trouble were an offence against his innocence.

Consequently suffering does not move man to prayer, but incites to anger, to a fist-shaking attitude of "I'll conquer nature! I'll not let her master me!" Then every new medical discovery is hailed as a new weapon against the supremacy of nature. And when at last men must admit that, after all, death is inescapable, they hold up their proud heads, making a vain glory of death. "A final, wonderful, blessed experience!"

That, they think, is far more heroic than the Christian's cry of rejoicing, "O Death, where is thy sting? O Grave, where is thy victory?"

By nature man resents pain and trouble. It angers him. He protests that it is unfair, and he does all in his power to keep it out of his life. And when it nevertheless enters, he

MAN VERSUS NATURE

is disillusioned. He becomes depressed and pessimistic. He may grit his teeth and bear it in stoical silence. Perhaps he tries to laugh it off. Or he feigns a certain satisfaction in endurance and a glorying in death.

To think and act so is to murmur against God.

The Word of God gives not the slightest ground for resentment against sickness and trouble. And by God's grace His people feel a strong aversion to that attitude. Oh, there may be moments when we, too, feel bitter because of the suffering that falls to our lot. Which of us does not at times fail? But the Holy Spirit within us witnesses against the momentary protest, and we are displeased with ourselves because of it.

Suffering is not escapable. We cannot banish it from our lives. That is beyond the power of man. We build dikes, tunnels, and dams; we invent telegraph and radio. But this is not a conquering of nature, nor does man thereby *prove how great he is*. Let a little volcanic tremor shake the earth, and where, O man, is your vaunted strength?

Man's conquest of nature rather consists in this, that when nature strives to undermine our efforts, to crush our hopes, to plunge us into misery and suffering, to return man to dust, then the Spirit of God within us spurs us on, gives us courage, hope and true heroism. He does not let us grow weary and faint and despairing. He strengthens us in and through that very suffering, that we may show before men and angels and demons how unconquerable is the man whose faith is in God. "Have faith as a mustard seed, and you shall bid the mountains remove into the sea."

It is indeed God's will that man shall wrestle against nature, and shall wrest a living from nature.

THE PRACTICE OF GODLINESS

In the many everyday little things we are constantly doing just that—in weeding our garden, in clothing ourselves, in averting death by means of food and drink and the general care of our bodies, until God Himself shall lay us in the dust.

In Old Testament days God taught His people many rules of clothing and cleanliness. Cleanliness is nothing less than another form of resistance to nature, a washing away of the soil and stain that tends to drag us to earth and infect us with disease.

God Himself commanded Noah to build the ark in preparation against the coming flood. And the rest of mankind was lost in the flood because they would not believe, and therefore would not avail themselves of the means of escape.

The Scriptures speak again and again of shelter in the time of storm, and protection against the raging elements. The seeking of such shelter is not condemned; instead, it is frequently mentioned as a symbol of man's seeking safety with God. Against the burning summer sun we seek shade, and when the blighting winter frosts come we make ourselves comfortable in our homes with fires and blankets.

Providing against future needs is as much a part of the struggle. And so are preventive measures. The Israelites were bidden to fence their roofs and stairways lest anyone fall. They dug pools on Zion's hills to preserve water for times of drought. And Jacob sent his sons to Egypt to buy corn from strangers in the time of famine.

Nowhere in Scripture do we find passive submission commended or recommended. Rather, there is a stimulation to put forth all our strength, to strive courageously against the destructive forces of nature, to protect life, to seek safety, to take preventative measures against trouble that is coming, or

MAN VERSUS NATURE

avert it if possible. Noah provided food for himself and for the animals in the ark. David defended himself and his flock against bear and lion, heroically fighting both.

And in regard to sickness, the Bible teaches the same preventative and protective attitude.

One of the most dreadful diseases among Israel was leprosy. The Lord did not let this dreadful scourge reign unchecked among His people. He gave detailed commands for diagnosis, treatment, isolation and disinfection.

When Israel was still in the wilderness, there were already apothecaries who made healing ointments. There was even an apothecaries' guild in Jerusalem. Hezekiah was treated with figs at the command of God. Jesus Himself said, "Those who are ill need a physician"—which clearly indicates that the skill of a physician is a gift of God's mercy. Luke, the evangelist-physician, whose pen has given us the beautiful details of the mysteries of Christ's birth, has hallowed the medical profession by appearing in the book of God as one of His special servants.

It is without doubt, then, that the herbs, many of them even poisonous, were intended for man's use against sickness. This implies that it is our duty to fight the ravages of diseases. There can be no other conclusion than this: God wills that we shall struggle, with the courage of faith and the strength of prayer, against every natural force that threatens health and life.

Epidemics and plagues are not excluded. Famine, too, is a scourge of God, and with pestilence frequently an aftermath of war. But Joseph was brought to Egypt, under the gracious provision of God, to prepare corn for the famine years. Prevention and precaution are not excluded, but included in the struggle against the enmity of nature.

THE PRACTICE OF GODLINESS

We may and must conclude that in general the afflictions which come upon us from nature, as well as those which Satan brings upon us, have one purpose—they are sent *in order that* we shall defend ourselves and protect our dear ones, in order that as we thus struggle on with courage, with zeal, heroically, we may through it all reveal the depth and the strength of our faith.

But the Word of God condemns unconditionally all seeking of medical help which excludes a seeking of the Lord, all use of preventatives and cures which disregards God, which fails to acknowledge Him as the giver of both the remedy and the wisdom to apply it. He who struggles against sickness and suffering without humbling himself in prayer and supplication before God, brings upon himself the curse of God. Not only the curse of Eden but a second curse comes upon the man who in foolish pride believes himself wise enough and strong enough and great enough to harness and subdue and control nature.

God's people have always protested against such godlessness, and they must continue to do so.

For the most meekly submissive Christian when he refuses medical aid because of true devotion to God, though he lacks understanding and is narrow in his conceptions, is nevertheless wiser and nobler than the man who, deeming himself too learned to believe in God, takes his medicine with the thought, "*I* shall conquer this sickness!"

No, we are not masters. We are creatures, wholly dependent, small, weak and helpless. All that we do is sin except it be done in faith.

In faith I put a lightning rod on my house; and when it catches the lightning from God's storm-clouds, to lead it

MAN VERSUS NATURE

away harmless, I thank God that I and my dear ones have escaped the danger. But without faith I have no surety. I cannot trust a ferry to carry me safely across the river, for God can cause a disaster which plunges me and my dear ones into death.

It is the will of God that, trusting Him, we protect our lives and the lives of our dear ones from all danger. He who fails to do what he can to rescue life is guilty of murder. He who neglects his own health or does not protect himself with the remedies which God provides, becomes guilty of suicide.

IV

Man Versus Man

War

WE have now come to the third question—what must be our reaction when men oppose us or injure us, or interfere with our holiest activities?

We shall begin our discussion with the worst manifestation of the struggle between men—war.

On the basis of God's Word, what must our attitude be toward war?

Every Christian hates war as a horrible slaughter of human life. But some object to war *as such,* believing that it is unlawful, and that he who makes war or participates in war is guilty before God.

There is within us a strong aversion to the very thought of shedding the blood of a fellowman.

But there is also a voice within us which says, "My honor above my life!"

If your child must have an arm amputated, you will go through agonies before you decide to say to the surgeon, "Go ahead." But such amputations are occasionally necessary. And a similar situation may arise among the nations. A nation may forfeit its honor or fail in its calling if it has not the courage to resist oppression and wrong.

Yet, there are those who say, "War? Never!"

MAN VERSUS MAN

They argue as follows:

"We must follow the example of Jesus, who 'when He suffered threatened not, but committed himself to him that judgeth uprightly.'

"And while it is true that in Old Testament times the Lord led His people into battle, we are living in a different age, a new dispensation.

"War is a denial of faith in God and His mercy and care. We are assured that 'all things work together for good to those who love God'—also the most cruel persecutions; and no one can be against us if God is for us. Therefore we may not resort to war to protect ourselves, even as Christ and His Apostles did not resist when they were persecuted.

"Even if someone should hatefully injure you or steal your worldly goods, you should do no more than try by friendliness and reason to induce him to desist from his wickedness, praying God meanwhile for help. As Paul says, 'Why not rather take the wrong? Why not rather be defrauded?'

"And if your life is in danger, flee, even as Paul did, praying for grace and courage that you may triumph in patience, following the example of the Lamb of God, Jesus Christ Himself, and of His disciples."

All of these arguments are based upon Scripture.

But these words of Scripture were not intended for governments and nations. They are, instead, injunctions intended for the life of God's people among each other. That is the great error of those who hold that all war is intrinsically sinful.

There were many conscientious objectors in the days of the Netherlands' war with Spain. And when the Beggars sailed in boldly and bravely to drive out the enemy, they condemned the action unconditionally. They clung to the conviction that man must not fight his own battles, but must sit still and wait for the direct intervention of the almighty Arm of God—by means of nature, or the angels, or His Spirit, but *not by means of men*.

Most whole-heartedly we would join them in the cry, "Not unto *us*, O Lord, but *to Thy Name* be the glory!" Yet we protest against the teaching that we must meekly wait for God's help without putting forth any effort of our own.

When the Lord blessed the rebellion against Spain, and subsequently built Himself a church in the Netherlands, men could no longer deny that He works directly through His people. It was too evident.

We must indeed submit to authority which God has ordained. "Obey them that have the rule over you, and submit yourselves." And "Let every soul be subject unto the higher powers. For there is no power but of God. The powers that be are ordained of God." Therefore what the government bids, you must do, even though it may seem unwise or unfair to you. If obedience requires no further sacrifice than that of comfort or money or pleasure, you are to obey. Implicitly.

On the contrary, if the government demands or commands something that is forbidden by God and His Church, then you may not obey.

You *may* not. God is the ruler over all. He has given authority to the powers that be. But their authority ends when *their* command runs contrary to *His*. They have no right to make any such requirements. In doing so, *they* become rebels against God.

MAN VERSUS MAN

Just where "rebellion of the authorities" begins is extremely difficult to say. Each of us must be convinced in his own heart, before his own Lord. And the Name of the Lord must never be used as a cloak for a rebellious spirit.

But supporting and abetting a government that rebels against the Lord of Hosts in demanding something contrary to His will, makes you, too, a rebel.

Under such circumstances, let there be passive resistance. What the government bids you do. you leave undone. Or what the government forbids, you do nevertheless, quietly and seriously, without fuss or display.

And if the authorities, moved to anger, cast you into prison, you must bear it. Should they take your life, you must submit, with eyes uplifted to the eternal reward.

All this, however, does not imply the exclusion of all war under all circumstances. Our church fathers held to four principles in regard to resistance against the authority.

First: Not every government has absolute authority. Frequently there are certain rights and privileges remaining to the people, by law or custom or tradition. When the government imposes its strength upon the subjects to take away these rights or in violation of these rights, it thereby forfeits its authority.

Second: Among most people there are leaders, lawfully appointed or elected, who are to protect the rights of the people against possible inroads of the government. These leaders retain their right and duty to defend the people, even against a government that has turned tyrannical.

Third: A nation may resist hired soldiers that are sent to destroy it.

Fourth: It may well be that God Himself calls a certain man, or a group, to lead in the resistance against tyranny.

THE PRACTICE OF GODLINESS

The Huguenots in France, the Covenanters in Scotland, the Beggars in the Netherlands—there can be no doubt that God called them to fight the enemies of God with the sword. Not one of the great church fathers has ever condemned their action in principle.

We will not go further into a study of Scripture on the subject. Others have done so most carefully and devoutly, and we respect the conclusions which they have reached, the more readily since with the Word of God in their hand they drove out the enemy to prepare a place for the church of God.

Politics

Just a few words about the attitude of God's people toward the politics of the nation.

There are those who feel that a Christian should not meddle in politics. Let the child of God care for his spiritual welfare, for his family, and for the little circle of Christians to which he belongs. But let him not become embroiled in political questions. Let Christians who would take the lead in political issues rather use their talents in evangelistic work. It were even well that we did not have to vote, did not have to choose representatives, had nothing at all to do with government.

People who hold such opinions have a deep realization of the fact that our sojourn on earth is but short, and that the fatherland above is our home, the place where our hearts long to be. They are convinced, too, that political struggles are useless; they claim to have historical proof that all this to-do and busy-ness is never productive of lasting results. And moreover, they protest that there is too much filth and crookedness about politics, so that no child of God can

MAN VERSUS MAN

meddle in political affairs without becoming contaminated and suffering spiritual loss.

Their attitude seems to be, "Let us leave the realm of politics to the world." For "Pure religion and undefiled before our God and Father is this, to visit the fatherless and the widows in their affliction, and to keep himself unspotted from the world."

But this is not the Christian view.

Neither was it the view or the practice of the Reformers.

A life of pious isolation and meditation was not their idea of obedience to God. They militated against such inactivity and passivity. And by the grace of God they were instrumental in stirring Christendom to new life and courage, in Switzerland, Netherlands, France and Scotland.

We can never accuse them of indifference to affairs of their country. They did not dream of leaving the reins of government in the hands of the world. In fact, the ideal of the reformers was a government within the church, the control of civic affairs under church supervision. They had no conception of separation between church and state as we now know it. Calvin and Zwingli were theocratic in their concept of church and politics.

The same ideas prevailed in France and Scotland in those days, and we might point to the Pilgrim Fathers of America as further evidence that our forebears did not shun politics.

Nor do we. For we believe that God's Word requires us to make our influence felt. And there is evidence of His blessing in the remarkable influence of the principles of reformed faith upon the history of people and nations.

Not that we should judge right and wrong by the results. For those who are on the side of right do not always triumph.

THE PRACTICE OF GODLINESS

In fact, they seldom do. Too frequently the wrong has the upperhand.

But we may not sit back, separating ourselves from national life, and expect the Lord to deliver us from oppression by a miracle from heaven.

He could do so. But that is not His pleasure.

Our God works by means. He uses men.

Therefore in the affairs of the nation, as well as in all other spheres of life, the Christian is called upon to fight the fight of faith, to be a soldier of Jesus Christ.

If we fail to obey the command of God, if we fail to defend the right, we shall suffer the downfall of the church and of our nation.

Exercising Authority

There are many relationships among men. One of them concerns the authority which some exercise over others.

Jesus said, "Judge not, that ye be not judged."

Does this imply, as some would have it, that we should not have courts of justice? That we should not punish evildoers, but instead should overlook as much as possible, and try to turn the evildoer from his wicked ways by kindness and gentleness? For what right has one man to judge another?

If we follow this suggestion to its logical conclusion, we shall have to condemn even the most palatial prison as too cruel; we may no longer frown upon our children when they do wrong; we must let evil have its way; and "whosoever shall smite thee on the right cheek, turn to him the left also."

But such a position is evidently untenable. It is also essentially contrary to God's Word, and a false interpretation.

MAN VERSUS MAN

It results from a confusion between the duty of private persons and the duty of magistrates.

To persons in private life Jesus spoke the injunction: Judge not, that ye be not judged. But He did not intend thereby to deny the right of human administration of justice. In fact, He himself honored and acknowledged both Jewish and Roman courts. Furthermore, Paul even recommended that there be judges in the church to settle disputes among Christians. And Paul also reminds us that the rulers do not bear the sword in vain.

We do well to distinguish carefully between private and official judging.

"Judge not, that ye be not judged"— what other rule of life could Christ give to creatures such as we are, wholly sinful, unworthy, condemnable, short-sighted and short-lived? The Holy Scripture shows you your utter unworthiness, leaves you nothing to boast of; and then necessarily teaches you not to be presumptuous, but to be humble and meek.

But that does not deprive a man of the authority which he may have by reason of his position. True, even the highest magistrate is a mere man, and in private life he is as insignificant and unworthy as any other man. As an officebearer, however, he is clothed with dignity, a dignity which does not emanate from himself but which is God-given. He has authority which God has entrusted to him, and which ought to glorify not himself but God.

Even Christians, and devout Christians, frequently fall short of honoring authority as it should be honored. This evil usually arises from a too high evaluation of self, as if *we* gave the authority to our leaders and therefore *we* may choose whether or not we shall recognize and obey

THE PRACTICE OF GODLINESS

that authority. That is a warped concept. Authority is derived from God; the person in authority is responsible to God only; and we owe him honor and respect because his authority is God's.

In general, we are willing to acknowledge the authority of our national leaders. But they are by no means the only ones who must be honored and obeyed. We owe respect to anyone, in any position of office, who has rightful claim to authority.

* * *

Fathers and mothers are in such a place of authority. They did not create their children; God made them. Nor do they own the children; they are God's. Neither may they demand obedience because they are stronger or more worthy than the children. The obedience of children to parents is a matter of *God's* honor and majesty. The child must obey his God—obey absolutely—because God is his Creator and Lord. And the parents have been endowed by God to represent *Him* and *His authority* toward the child.

Therefore disobedience should be punished not first of all because it is bothersome to the parents, or because the child may otherwise be spoiled, but first of all and principally because the child's disobedience is *opposition to God*.

That is the reason why parents must discipline and chastise the child and must insist upon obedience. Even when they are moved with pity, even though they know that their own sins and inconsistencies have affected the child, yet they may not neglect the responsibility of asserting their authority.

A mother may be frail, may be a widow, and her son may be a young giant, yet he is and must be subject to her, and must obey her for God's sake.

MAN VERSUS MAN

Our civil laws support the parents in this, for they give parents the right even to put a child in detention if necessary.

We may not say, "Just let it pass!" or "Oh, all children are like that nowadays." We may not think, "I'd rather avoid trouble and a scene." Parents are in duty bound to uphold the honor of God by demanding obedience. Note —not *their* honor, but God's. *That* is why indulgence or leniency is sin.

This does not mean, of course, that parents should be stern and hard. There is need of wisdom, discretion, and careful justice: and we should take into account extenuating circumstances. But right must triumph, even in the life of a child. The child must obey — if not willingly, then unwillingly.

One thing, however, we must add in all earnestness: be sure that your child feels that you are punishing him not because *you* are angry, but because *God's* anger rests upon sin. Let him realize that you yourself are deeply and penitently conscious of your own guilt before God.

• • •

There are others in authority — in the shop, in the office, at school, in societies — and they, too, are called upon to exercise their authority.

Too often leaders do all in their power to make paths smooth and to avoid trouble. We seek our ease. Or perhaps we are cowardly; we do not want to, or do not dare to, face opposition and anger. We would rather just keep still and let the matter go its way. Often our guiding thought is: How can I best keep peace? When it should be: What is right? According to the Word of God, what ought to be done?

For obedience is better than sacrifice.

God has so ordered human relationships that there are those who command and those who obey. He who is in command must take his task seriously, for he is responsible to God for honest and fair exercise of his authority — whether he be a king, or a chairman of a meeting, or a foreman in a factory. Authority is not a pretty plaything, nor is it honorary ornament. It is a duty.

* * *

We must not forget that there is a distinction between one's behavior as a private person and his behavior as having authority. Too often the tables are strangely turned. People who are vested with authority are apt to be lax in their official duties and hesitant in enforcing the right, yet they will assert themselves vigorously in private life. In their positions as leaders when they should be firm in the cause of right, they are pliable and easily swayed. But as private persons, when Jesus' command of meekness and tolerance applies to them, they easily take offence, they are irritable and self-willed, and quick to assert their rights.

Thus God's order is reversed.

In the exercise of rightful authority, not *our* honor but *God's* is at stake; and we are prone to be indifferent or we lack the necessary courage. In private life, when our personal honor is threatened, we bristle with quick resentment.

Such calls down upon us the judgment of God. For He is a jealous God, jealous also of His honor.

V

The Church of Jesus Christ

Doctrines of the Church

THE subject of differences in doctrine within the church has been discussed at length by theologians and church leaders.

The question is this: Cannot two different doctrines be held within a church? Ought we not to allow for differences? Should we not be tolerant, and cover up or ignore these points of difference in order to keep peace? Cannot we at least moderate the differences and keep them within bounds?

As always, we seek the answer in God's Word. *There* we find bounds within which we must stay.

There are three phases to be considered: our own attitude in regard to such differences, the points of difference themselves, and to persons with whom we differ.

As to our attitude—we may not let personal interests or any feeling of animosity toward those who differ with us mingle with our zeal in defense of the truth. We are to hate all untruth and evil for *God's* sake, and try to win back to the right path those who have strayed.

When Moses dashed the tables of the law to pieces on the mount, and ground the golden calf to powder, he was not giving vent to his personal bitter anger, but was expressing

THE PRACTICE OF GODLINESS

zeal for God. This is evident from the fact that he begged to have his name removed from God's book rather than that God should bring dishonor upon His Holy Name by destroying the Israelites. Paul demands the same attitude of every servant of Christ when he writes to Timothy (II Tim. 2:24) "And the servant of the Lord must not strive but be gentle unto all men, apt to teach, patient, in meekness instructing those that oppose themselves, if God peradventure will give them repentance to the acknowledging of the truth..." And further, "Preach the word; be instant in season, out of season, reprove, rebuke, exhort with all longsuffering and doctrine" (II Tim. 4:2). These words do not teach indolence or indifference or silence toward the beliefs of others; but they do insist that in all protest against false doctrine the motivation should not be personal feeling but the glory of God and the edification of our fellowmen, also of those with whom we differ.

The points of difference must also be considered, whether or not they concern fundamental doctrine. Where there is difference of interpretation of a certain passage of Scripture and no fundamental doctrine is involved, there should be tolerance. One may have his own opinion without denying another his. For the Christian reader is free to accept that interpretation which he, guided by the Holy Spirit dwelling within him, deems the most nearly correct. This is part of the liberty of the children of God. For we know only in part, and we prophecy in part, because we see but dimly. And through the variety of opinions the meaning frequently becomes more clear in due time.

But if the interpretation is such that it contradicts an article of faith, then it must be refuted, for the truth of the Gospel must be defended against all false doctrine.

THE CHURCH OF JESUS CHRIST

Take for example, Christ's statement in John 14:28, "My Father is greater than I." Some interpret this as referring to His human nature; others say Jesus spoke of His state of humiliation; still others take it to mean that in becoming obedient to His Father as our Mediator, Christ humbled himself. Neither of the three is in conflict with our confessions. But if the text should be interpreted to mean that Christ here disclaims divinity, that He denies His essential oneness with the Father, then we are faced with a doctrine that conflicts with the confession that Christ is true and eternal God. Such differences cannot be tolerated within the church.

Finally in regard to the persons who are led away by false opinions and doctrines. There are two kinds—those who are new or weak in the faith, and those who are strong and who covertly or openly defend their ideas and strive to win other adherents. The first must be dealt with gently, and taught a fuller measure of truth, that they may grow in faith. We must bear with those who are weak.

But toward those who believe and teach doctrines not in accordance with the Word of God we cannot be tolerant. We must defend the truth earnestly, in order that if possible they may be won back, or that they may at least be warned of their error. The full counsel of God should be expounded to them simply and clearly.

Tolerance and forbearance, then, must indeed characterize us in our personal attitude, and where minor differences are concerned, and in our forbearance toward those who are new or weak in the faith.

But those who teach anything contrary to the Word of God cannot remain in the church of God.

THE PRACTICE OF GODLINESS

Peace at Any Price?

The articles of Christian faith are like links of a chain. If one link is removed, the chain is broken. For instance, one cannot deny God's eternal election without taking away our assurance of salvation and undermining the steadfastness of our hope. For then man's salvation is left in his own hands; he must exercise his free will and choose to be saved. That, in turn, denies at least in part man's depravity. And if man is not totally depraved, Christ's atonement loses much of its value — in fact we would finally arrive at the conclusion that we do not need Christ for salvation!

Furthermore, if we should hush certain doctrines, we are suppressing the truth. If we hide differences under a broad creed that permits of two or more interpretations, as some suggest, we hide truth and leave men in uncertainty. We may not tamper with truth.

Satan knows that he can undermine the structure of the church by slyly removing just one fundamental doctrine at a time, and he frequently loosens a large foundation stone gradually, chiselling it away bit by bit.

That is why tolerance for the sake of peace may be dangerous.

There are those who plead for tolerance in order that others may be drawn to the fold and thus the Name of God may receive greater honor. Ought we not, they say, join hands and thus unite the now so sadly divided Christendom? Can we not forget disputes? Minimize our differences? And thus increase our strength?

Theirs is a beautiful and worthy ideal, to unite the children of God under one roof. It ought indeed to be our

THE CHURCH OF JESUS CHRIST

purpose and desire. But how? Shall we try to cure ills by means of a greater ill? Must we have peace at any price? Shall each give in a little? Tone down doctrines and forget differences?

Paul did not compromise with the Galatian adherence to the law by toning down his teaching of free grace! Quite the opposite! He reprimanded them for giving heed to false doctrine, and sought to lead them back to the truth

If the principles of our faith are man-made, they should be discarded. If they are from God, let no man tamper with them to tone them down. Even though some points may seem to be but small, God has bidden us be faithful in little things, and has forbidden that we subtract even one iota from His Word.

One step toward giving in will lead to a next step. And will not God visit us with blindness if we deliberately darken the truth He has graciously entrusted to us? How shall we justify ourselves if we permit even a little of the truth to be laid aside? Is that *ours* to do?

* * *

Moreover, there can be no *real* and *lasting* peace in the church of God without full harmony of opinions and belief. If doctrines were so toned down and moderated that they were capable of more than one interpretation, those who differed in opinion would still argue and each would do all he could to uphold and spread his own interpretation. For what a man conscientiously accepts as truth, he desires others to believe also. The false unity would not last.

We must indeed seek peace, with all earnestness. Bitterness, ill will, malice, and love of dispute should never characterize a Christian in his defense of the truth. Instead,

there should be a sincere interest in the honor of God and in the well-being of our fellowmen. Paul says, "As much as lieth in you, live peaceably with all men."

But when he says, "As much as lieth in you" he plainly implies that sometimes peace is impossible. When peace is injurious to the truth, peace must give way. Peace with God is of greater value than peace with men. To desire peace at the expense of truth is hypocrisy and weakness — and highly displeasing to God.

Having then purified your souls in obeying the truth through the spirit, unto unfeigned love of the brethren, see that ye love one another with a pure heart fervently. Walk worthy of the vocation wherewith ye are called, with all lowliness and meekness, with longsuffering, forbearing one another in love; endeavoring to keep the unity of the Spirit in the bond of peace.

And the God of mercy and peace, the God of order and unity, grant that we may be of one mind and may together praise Him in unity of faith, now and eternally.

The Imperfection of the Church

There is nothing among men that is as it ought to be. Nothing has remained as God made it. Everything is out of joint; everywhere there is confusion. Sin shook the very foundation of human life, and therefore the walls are cracked and bowed and askew.

The church of Christ does not stand apart, separate from all the disruption and wreckage of the sin-cursed world. Christ gathers His church within that world, and its members are all sinners. Every one of them is imperfect.

Yes, in principle they are perfect, through Jesus Christ; but by no means are they perfect in daily living and doing.

THE CHURCH OF JESUS CHRIST

Even the holiest of Christians struggles till his dying day against the weakness and sinfulness of his heart.

Because the church of Christ is a gathering of imperfect people, it is an imperfect church. The church is holy because Christ is its head; it has beauty because Christ adorns it; it has heavenly gifts and powers. But it is mired in sin, and the filth of sin clings to it.

Not only the lay members, but the leaders as well are sinful. All are men of like passions. And the leaders, because of their position, must guard against the temptation to vainglory and spiritual pride. Worthy though their office is, it does not exempt them from the grip of sin. They stumble even while they reach out a hand to help others. They are shepherds not because of their own virtues and qualifications, but because the Lord bids them bring His Word and guide the footsteps of His people.

If all the members of the church are imperfect, it follows that even the outward forms, the organization, the management, the activities and the usages cannot but be faulty. How can the walls be strong when the stone is brittle and the cement is weak?

Throughout all the centuries God has had to labor with His people. Was there ever a time, in any age of history, when the church was truly beautiful, pure, free from spot or blemish? In the days of the apostles things already began to go wrong. Their epistles are full of complaints and warnings against sins and false doctrines.

We Christians of today ought to take this fact to heart, fully realizing that the imperfection and weakness of today's church is not at all unusual or unnatural.

Could we perhaps, by better cooperation and greater zeal, bring about a perfect and glorious church?

THE PRACTICE OF GODLINESS

Whoever thinks so, underrates the extent of evil in human nature and deceives himself.

Yet there are those who dream this dream and who burn with eager desire to bring about its fulfilment. They are deeply conscious of the great and holy calling of the church, and they are grieved by its failings, its shameful weakness. To cure the ills seems to them a hopeless task. So the like-minded band together and form a new church or a society, where they may enjoy richer and purer spiritual fellowship of kindred hearts. And thus their dream seems to come true.

But it will not last.

They attain to their happy condition by separating the more pure from the less pure, but that is not a normal situation. While they seem to have excluded much evil from their small circle, and to have escaped dangerous contamination, they soon find that evil came in with them; it is among them; the age-old evil raises its horrid head among even the most consecrated and separated. The dream of a perfect church on earth is a vain dream.

Besides such dreamers in the church, there are also those who, equally aware of the evils, and equally grieved over them, are wide awake and know from God's Word and from history that a healthy church is a rarity and a pure church is an impossibility. They know that there is not one shred of prophecy which even hints at possible perfection of the church of Christ. They realize that they have no right to expect such a church. They would fight evil, yes. But expect perfection? **No.**

Sin is a destroyer that creeps in everywhere. Therefore we must expect an imperfect church. In fact, we church members carry the sin of the world with us into the church, too often hiding it under a veil of spirituality!

THE CHURCH OF JESUS CHRIST

If the church were not the Bride of His Son, surely God would in holy wrath destroy not first of all the world, but rather first of all the wretched sin-ridden church.

We have mentioned these two kinds of church members — those who dream of a perfect church and those who soberly face the fact of her inevitable imperfection. But let us not carry away the idea that the two classes are always clearly distinguishable. The dreamer has his moments of sober insight, and the man who calmly accepts the fact of evil also dreams his dreams. Men are far more alike than we often think. Where is the believer who does not have a spectre of unbelief crouching within his heart? Where is the man who, while he professes salvation by free grace, does not find himself secretly priding in good works? Even the child of God who believes in free will and despises the doctrine of particular grace bows humbly before his God in his inner chamber, confessing his utter helplessness and unworthiness before his Maker.

But in one man this has the upper hand, and in another that.

Our purpose is not to honor the one and upbraid the other. Rather, we would analyze and understand the holy things of God, in order that we may come to the truth; that untruth may fall away; that thus through the work of the Holy Spirit, God's Name may receive the greater honor.

It is possible to have sinful ideals, ideals that reach out for more than God has seen fit to give us and that indicate a dissatisfaction with God's decrees. The dream of a perfect church upon earth is such an ideal. The imperfection of God's church upon earth is a circumstance which we must accept and bear with patience. If we fail to see that, it is because we fail to see the satanic depths of sin, and fail

THE PRACTICE OF GODLINESS

to realize that the church is in its very essence inseparable from the sinfulness of man.

Fighting the Good Fight

Those who cherish the idea of a pure church on earth frequently urge as special incentive the imminent return of Christ. Since He is at the very door, they say, we must break away from this earthly life and go to meet Him.

We must indeed live in the consciousness that Jesus may come tomorrow, or may even appear upon the clouds tonight. The disciples themselves were ever aware of the nearness of His coming. For them eternity did not lie at the end of time, but is now; Eternity is the very ground, the foundation, upon which Time rests.

But we must not err in striving *to meet the Lord* instead of patiently awaiting His coming.

If the Lord is to come as a thief in the night, the church should go about its daily duties in quiet devotion, until He suddenly appears. We are not to keep looking out the window, or climbing to the housetops to gaze eagerly into the distance, while neglecting our work and giving our household duties but scant attention.

Indeed we must watch. We must so live that we are ready to welcome Him at any moment. Like a Christian family that, having commended home and children to God's care for the night, quietly goes to bed and to sleep, and awakens in the morning to resume the daily task, so the church of Christ upon earth must go on quietly, prayerfully, with its common daily tasks, until He comes, in His own time, to break off this round of daily duties.

A deep and living faith in God's Covenant is the foundation of our quiet, watchful, patient waiting and working.

THE CHURCH OF JESUS CHRIST

For included in God's covenant are also all the chosen who are yet to be brought into the fold, though they may now be drunkards, or thieves, or self-righteous rejectors of the truth. They are destined to be saved; and it is through the ministration of the church that they must be brought to the light and taught in the truth.

This one confession, that God is God, and that He will bring in His own, makes us patient to bear with the imperfections and weaknesses of the church, since He has seen fit to place that cross upon us. And it also keeps us humble before Him, as we must confess our own guilt. "The sin of the church is also my sin. I, yea even especially I, am at fault."

Not one of us will then blame the world or the indifference of fellow-Christians for the evils of the church, saying, "*I am a zealous laborer in the Lord's vineyard! I am not guilty of this coldness and indifference! I shall lead the way to perfection!*"

That holier-than-thou attitude is sinful and abhorrent.

But, being keenly aware of his own sins, and knowing full well that he has fanned the flames of sin perhaps more than others, the true Christian fights against sin the more earnestly and zealously.

* * *

Fight we must, constantly, without rest. Every child of God is a soldier of Jesus Christ, called as were the Levites of old *to war the warfare of the Lord.* And every office bearer must know that as he takes office he *enters into that warfare.*

It is a warfare *for* God, *against* Satan. It is a participation in the war which God himself wages against Satan, and which God's holy angels wage against Satan's angel-hosts.

THE PRACTICE OF GODLINESS

The war of the world against the King of glory. The war of the spirit against flesh. War within us and without. War which emanates from God and is directed against the might of Satan, the world, death, sin, deceit, and the lusts of the flesh.

Therefore it is a war of every one who is anointed with the Holy Spirit. He must fight with Christ, for Christ, and under the leadership of Christ.

It is a war of which Paul testifies, "I have fought the *good fight*, I have kept the faith, henceforth there is laid up for me a crown of righteousness, which the Lord, the righteous judge, shall give me in that day."

It is evident, then, that there can be no true zeal for the church without spiritual warfare against sin.

Zeal for the church, however pious it may appear to be, is abominable hypocrisy if it goes hand in hand with neglect of spiritual warfare against such enemies of God as lying, uncleanness, self-righteousness, cold-heartedness.

Some there are who pretend to be faithful watchmen upon Zion's walls but harbor such sins in their own hearts, or overlook them in their children and fellow-church members.

They are *un*faithful.

For they allow the enemy free play within. They cry out against the danger of the wolf howling outside the walls, while a pack of wolves is busily devouring the sheep within!

That is not real devotion to the cause of Christ. Nor does it reveal true faith.

* * *

The battle for the Lord must begin *within ourselves;* only then can it kindle outward and be sincerely waged with equal fervor against enemies all around.

THE CHURCH OF JESUS CHRIST

Our impassioned battle cry must ever be: Friend or enemy! All that is from the Evil One is your enemy, everywhere and in all forms—in your flesh, in your thoughts, in your very virtues, in the disrupted social conditions, in the schools—lower as well as higher—in your homes, and also in the church of your Lord.

Are you zealous for the church with great enthusiasm, while neglecting the evils which creep into your home, your friendships, your social life, and worst of all neglecting to fight your own personal spiritual battles? Then you are living a lie.

To "war the warfare of the Lord" and to "keep the watch of the house of the Lord" is to battle in every sphere, in every manner, in all relationships; every moment, always and everywhere standing against Satan, always and everywhere and in everything on the side of God.

Many will be ashamed upon reading this, even as our own soul bows in shame at the writing.

For who of us would dare say that his own hands are clean for the battle?

But let that not dishearten! For we *must* feel ashamed. God's Word must bring upon us, again and again, a conviction of sin that burns as a fire into our very inmost being.

Only let us take care that our principles remain founded upon the true foundation.

If we fight for the church of God and neglect the evil within our own hearts, however men may attempt to justify such action, we incur the judgment of God.

When we acknowledge our own guilt, acknowledge the justice of the accusation against our false zeal, then pardon is assured us. And the Lord our God will lead us on.

THE PRACTICE OF GODLINESS

Each must ask himself: Does my zeal for the church flow from my inner battle against sin and Satan?

He who truly takes up the fight against sin and Satan in his own heart and in his personal life, must necessarily fight sin and Satan in the church also.

He who looks on unconcernedly while untruth and sin grow rampant within the church of his Lord is also weak, half-hearted and sickly in his own spiritual struggle.

The good fight must be fought in every sphere. *In* the church and *without*. Wherever the shadow of Satan falls, the soldier of the Lord is called to prompt action.

Obedience

The motives of all you do and strive to do may never be found in your desires, but always and unconditionally in the Lord.

As long as your complaints about the church, and your efforts to improve the church, are motivated by *self*, because the imperfections annoy *you* or displease *you*, and because the church falls short of *your* ideals, then you are on the wrong path.

Then, if your efforts fail, you will grumble because your needs are not filled and your rights are not honored. And eventually you will perhaps withdraw yourself as from something unworthy of your labors.

But once you realize that *not my honor* but the *honor of God* is the true motive for the battle against evil, then the beauty of simple obedience will become clear to you. Then you will no longer say, "The church must change because I cannot endure this lack of consecration." But you will say, "I may not be idle, for I am in the service of my God, who

THE CHURCH OF JESUS CHRIST

commands me to battle incessantly and undauntedly against the desecration of His church."

Then, too, it no longer matters if there are no immediate results upon your efforts and protests against evil. *That makes no difference at all.*

For you realize that you have no right or claim to a model church. You acknowledge yourself a humble sinner whose imperfections add to the corruption of the church.

Whether you live to see the church sink deeper into the mire, or to see it lifted to higher planes *makes no difference.* You are in duty bound to defend her against her enemies all the days of your life, with all of God's children.

You obey. God bids you labor in His vineyard, and you do so with all the strength He gives you. He bids you not to sit with the scoffers and the ungodly, and you separate yourself from them. He bids you resist the onslaughts of evil upon His house, and you resist them.

When you have learned thus to obey, the battle for the Lord goes on without pause, yet calmly and steadily. It is a labor that looks not upon the results.

You are no longer striving for what *you* want or deem necessary; you are not impatient, not wearied with complaining or unmanned by disappointment. You simply obey. You are not less zealous, but more; not less constant, but more persevering.

And God, who is merciful, will crown your efforts, in home and heart and church, with His blessing.

* * *

By nature we crave freedom. We say, "I shall be master of my fate!" and "I shall do as I please." We chafe under

THE PRACTICE OF GODLINESS

rules and laws. Hence we also protest that the church must not interfere with individual self-expression.

And by nature we are also inclined to slothfulness. It is so much more pleasant to sit idle than to exert ourselves! We love our ease.

Imagine the activity, the upheavals, the changes, the disruptions that would ensue if all Christians obediently put into actual practice the will of Christ! We admire the men of old who gave their all and dared to risk their very lives. But our admiration seldom produces willingness to part with our own earthly possessions.

The craving for freedom, plus the distaste for exertion and danger, make it easy for us to accept the teaching: "Sit still and see what the Lord will do."

But we should be up and doing. And the Word says, "Whatsoever your hand findeth to do, do it with all your might." And, "All who would live godly lives shall suffer persecution."

May He, before whom we humbly confess our own guilt and for whose Name and honor we have striven also in the writing of these essays, use our words to open the eyes of many to their calling as members of the church of Jesus Christ.

PART II

CHRISTIAN PATIENCE

"Let us run with patience the race that is set before us."

HEBREWS 12:1.

CHRISTIAN PATIENCE

I

Patience a Rarity

PATIENCE is a very desirable possession, a precious treasure. It is a gift of God to the broken-hearted.

Patience is not a common possession. We rarely meet with it, but it is frequently confused with imitations called "submissiveness" and "resignation."

Patience does not sparkle in the sunlight of the day. It glows in the darkness, with an inner light. It glows in the night of suffering—of physical suffering, but especially of spiritual suffering, when the soul wrestles in deepest distress.

Patience is not like a beautiful climbing rose that twines its blossom-laden branches about the cross of life; it is rather like the modest spice-bush, without beauty of form or color, which perfumes the air with pungent sweetness.

Patience is like the nightingale, that has no beauty of plumage but sings sweetly in the dark night.

Or it is a precious stone which has no luster until the skilled worker has cut and ground and polished it.

Patience is one of the holy adornments with which Jesus Himself adorns the soul after He has cleansed it with His righteousness.

Christian patience has little in common with its namesakes found among men and women who live as "good neighbors" but are strangers to the grace of God. For in the heart that is not born anew true patience cannot grow. Such a heart has not the needed soil, and the atmosphere of the unsanctified life tends rather to wither it. A light brighter than the light of the sun, light from God Himself, unfolds its blossoms.

Patience is a fruit of the Spirit.

Its seed is not within us.

Its branches twine about the cross of Christ. Its goal is eternity. Its glory is in the grace of God.

Patience ought to be the possession of every child of God. If it is not his when he is reborn, it ought to grow within him as he grows in Christ.

But it is sadly lacking among us.

That is evident from our restlessness, from our aversion to the cross, though we hide that aversion behind a veil of resignation. It is especially evident when suffering fails to produce spiritual fruit, even suffering that is drained to the bitter dregs with apparent willingness.

We need patience. We need it to comfort us in trouble, to renew in us the joy of being God's children, to revive our song of praise as we bear the cross which His love assigns us.

Then shall not God's people lend willing ears to what the Word has to say about patience?

WE GLORY IN STRENGTH

II

We Glory in Strength

BY NATURE man is averse to patience. By nature man admires that which is strong and vigorous and powerful.

This is true not only of the man to whom the world is all. We Christians, too, because of the natural man within us, tend to enjoy a display of strength, and we watch with breathless interest when there is an exhibition of great power.

The ancients gloried in the games of the arena, where strength was pitted against strength. And how they worshipped the proud winner! That was not heathenish; it was human—human according to the standards of fallen man.

Today we still burn incense to our heroes and idolize them. We build monuments to those who fought great battles and performed valiant deeds. The human heart is ever ready to praise one who can do and dare, one who excels in physical prowess or in mental genius, one who keeps us spellbound by his daring and courage.

Such hero-worship is found among children at play, among young people at school, and among adults as well.

The idea of "a lamb that is dumb before the shearer" has no appeal to the world.

Stephen kneeling meekly under the rain of stones does not thrill men.

"Turn him thy left cheek also" is folly to them.

THE PRACTICE OF GODLINESS

Patience is despised.
Energy! Power! Strength! In these man glories.

* * *

And rightly!
For in this, as in all things, man is groping for the real and the true. With its little remaining instinct, man's sinful natural unregenerated heart always reaches out hungrily for reality and truth. But it does not seek them in God. Therefore when man thinks to climb upward, he is plunging downward. He clutches at an ideal and grasps an imitation, a sham.

So the child of God, too, desires and admires power. For true strength and power belong to Him who is the All-powerful, the Almighty; to His Son, who brought life to the dead; to the Spirit who, emanating from the Father and the Son, renews the face of the earth.

Strength is the glory of a Christian—strength to fight, to wrestle, to endure.

The devout child of God, who walks close to his God, protests against "submissiveness." Meek submission is contrary to the Word, contrary to the very nature of godliness, a failure to recognize the very essence of the Spirit.

Submissiveness is not a fruit of grace. It is rather an effort to earn favor.

How often a sufferer is told to "submit to the will of God," to be "resigned," to be meek and humble under the hand of God!

But that is not what God's Word means when it exhorts to patience.

True patience is not meek submission to the inevitable, or apathetic drifting without resistance.

WE GLORY IN STRENGTH

True patience, Biblical patience, is energy, buoyancy. It is strength—a strength more than earthly in origin.

It is *endurance*.

True patience is a mystery. Only the initiated can understand it. Only in faith can we attain to it.

Consider how two men accept inescapable suffering. One fears the pain and eagerly avails himself of the anesthetic which will make him insensible to the cutting knife. He does not want to suffer. He submits, but refuses to feel the pain. The other wants to know what is going on. Though the pain will be severe, he steels himself to bear it; he remains keenly sensitive to the knife, and endures the pain without complaint or moan. His is not mere submission. It is endurance.

Endurance is an exercise of heroic strength.

Have you experienced this higher strength, the strength of Christian patience?

III

For Love of God

HAVE you exhorted the sick and suffering to be patient and calm? Have you comforted them with talk of resignation, of submission to the will of God? Or praised them for bearing their cross without complaint?

Perhaps so. For such seems to be the accepted and common words of those who seek to comfort, uttered most earnestly by the sincere child of God as well as by those who have drifted from Him.

Yet such comfort is not in accordance with the spirit of God's Word.

In His Word we do not read of "resignation" or "submission," or of reconciling oneself to one's lot.

Such ideas come from the Stoics of ancient Greece and from the fatalistic Mohammedan's creed.

One who suffers without complaint may do so for the sake of the *world,* or for love of *self,* or for love of *God.* And only the last is true patience.

A soldier may be spurred to bravery by thirst for gain or honor. Pride and self-love may give him strength to bear hardship and pain without a murmur. Thus he may triumph over his suffering—triumph without faith in God, perhaps even while mocking at God and religion.

The stoics of ancient Greece and the fatalistic Mohammedans have their counterpart among us, even among us Chris-

FOR LOVE OF GOD

tians. There are men who control themselves with rigid discipline, as if they were above suffering and sorrow. They pride themselves on being strong characters. They are ashamed to give way to grief or even to show any emotion. In secret they may occasionally writhe in pain or despair; in the presence of others never.

But their strength is not in God. It is in self, in their own enthroned ego.

There are others, among the common run of folk, who submit to suffering as inevitable. It is the will of God, they say. And they confuse the scriptural doctrine of predestination with fatalism. It would be useless to protest or murmur. They resign themselves to trouble as a prisoner resigns himself to the narrow confines of his cell. They swallow their resentment. They sigh apathetically.

Thus men deaden themselves to feeling. They deaden themselves to love and beauty as well as to suffering. They kill within themselves the capacity to suffer, and they crush the heart's craving for the lost happiness of Paradise. When the storms of life beat upon them and the waves of trouble wash over their heads, they shut their eyes and stop their ears—they choose rather to sink to near oblivion than to suffer. By living less, they suffer less.

Men who deny the Christ can thus make a show of noble strength without dependence upon the Source of all strength. In their show of noble courage they ignore Him who sends the suffering. They bear it in the strength of their own pride, hardening their hearts, stifling all feeling.

And then man says, in his pride, that one can overcome sorrow without the Man of Sorrows, and one can triumph over death without the help of Him who conquered death.

THE PRACTICE OF GODLINESS

Then they tell of the sick, how quiet and resigned they are upon their beds, though godless; how calmly and peacefully they die! They tell it tauntingly, because we still dare to confess that there is no peace apart from God!

And we who confess that great truth are to blame for this taunt of the godless. Because we, with the Word of God in our very homes, have helped to dim the light which Jesus shed upon the mystery of suffering. We have slipped back into the attitude of the ignorant heathen. We, too, enthrone proud self-control. And then we imagine that we are thus honoring God! It may even be that we label a deathbed "Christian" when it has no other virtue than that of stoical resignation to the inevitable. In so doing, we make it possible for the non-Christian to say, "We too can die thus; we can die thus *without* the Christ!" .

Indeed they can die thus, and live thus too—calm, patient, submissive. Like the bones of Ezekiel's valley of the dead. But that is not *life*. That is not the life that throbs within you if you are one of those upon whom Christ has breathed life, if you are rejoicing in life from the dead! It is not being sensitive, as was tender Jesus.

The mystery of Christian suffering is not a dulling of sensitivity, nor a shrinking from pain, nor a wearing of complete armor about the flesh and heart so that no arrow can penetrate and no sword can pierce the inner recesses. But for Jesus' sake the Christian is willing to suffer, willing even to bear the added burden which will be his because he confesses Christ, knowing that just because he is a child of God he must endure the chastisement of a Father.

The Christian does not invite suffering. Neither does he struggle through it tearlessly when it comes. He pleads that

FOR LOVE OF GOD

it may be shortened; but in the midst of suffering he rises above his distress with a holy joy and a psalm of praise.

How is this possible?

The apostle says that though you give your body to be burned and have not love, your suffering would be in vain.

Only the glowing warmth of love can fuse intense suffering and exalted joy into a song of praise unto God.

The question then is this: Do you suffer *for love of God?* Suffer so, that you are drawn nearer to Him? Becoming even more His, and He yours? Are you, as it were, tearing your way through the thorns and thistles of life toward the gate of the Kingdom to meet Him, your God?

Such love does not originate within us.

"Love is of God." It is shed forth into our hearts only through the Holy Spirit whom He has sent.

THE PRACTICE OF GODLINESS

IV

A Strength of the Spirit

PATIENCE is not submissiveness; nor is it resignation to fate; nor is it stoical apathy.

What then is the nature of patience? What is the secret of patience in the new life of a Christian?

We would describe it thus: Patience is a strength of spirit, engendered within the heart of God's children by the Holy Spirit, which enables them to remain standing, unshaken and undaunted, in spite of all the forces that would tear them from the Kingdom of God.

It is *strength;* it is *endurance.*

The child of God has a new life, a life not of this world, a life supernaturally implanted within him by a mighty act of God. And he lives that new life, though he himself does not understand it, by the strength of the Holy Spirit who, having instilled it, also sustains and preserves it.

Because this new life within the Christian is of God, it is opposed to Satan, sin, and the world. Therefore Satan cannot and does not let it grow unhindered. In self-defense and in hatred against God he attacks God's children, striving to crush that new life lest it crush and undermine his power. That is why he attacks the freeborn of the Lord so zealously, now with cunning and slyness, often openly, and always without quarter. Sometimes he uses wily temptation as a weapon. Sometimes he works through the secret deep-seated sins of character. Sometimes he throws our once-forgiven sins into our faces. At times he pours over us a veritable flood of adversity and spiritual agony.

A STRENGTH OF THE SPIRIT

Thus the life of a Christian becomes a struggle, a constant struggle to remain standing against the onslaughts of Satan.

And the strength which enables a child of God to come through the terrible fray unharmed, to stand fast without giving way an inch, is called *patience,* or *endurance.*

The Greek word which the apostle uses literally means: *to remain in the position in which one is placed.* That is, to stay at one's post, to stand fast.

Again and again the apostles used the contest of the arena to illustrate the Christian's life in the world. These contests, especially the Olympic games, were regarded as the noblest test of a man's honor and strength. To be crowned a victor in the Olympic games was the highest distinction a Greek could win. And the whole populace praised and extolled the hero, with highest enthusiasm.

Thus it is no wonder that Paul frequently speaks of the games. "Brethren, I count not myself to have laid hold; but one thing I do, forgetting the things which are behind, and stretching forward to the things which are before, I press on toward the goal unto the prize of the high calling of God in Christ Jesus." And again, "Henceforth there is laid up for me the crown of righteousness, which the Lord, the righteous judge, shall give me at that day; and not to me only, but also unto all them that have loved his appearing."

To the Corinthians he writes, "Know ye not that they that run in a race run all, but one receiveth the prize? And every man that striveth in the games exerciseth self-control in all things. Now they do it to receive a corruptible crown; but we an incorruptible. I therefore so run as not uncertainly; so fight I as not beating the air; but I buffet my body and bring it to bondage. . . ."

THE PRACTICE OF GODLINESS

In these Olympic games there was a contest for runners, a race-track for horses drawing handsome three-wheelers, and an arena where man wrestled with man. Such an arena Paul has in mind when he says (Romans 5), "Tribulation worketh steadfastness"—that is, *endurance*, or *patience*.

Since the Olympic games were tournaments of honor, no one was permitted to take part without first submitting to a two-fold examination: his reputation in society, and his physical health must be approved. To ascertain the first, a crier was sent through the streets, calling upon anyone who might have a charge against him to speak up, for the honor of Greece. If a man was found to be in debt, or a slave, or guilty of some misdeed, all this was made public to his shame, and he was barred from the arena. But if he was a freeman, and his record was clear, the crier would lead him through the streets with honor and so admit him to the arena.

Paul, in the afore-mentioned chapter, glories in the fact that we, children of God, have not been denied admission to the arena. Our debts have been paid and we have been cleared of all accusations, through faith in Jesus Christ whose blood has made us freemen. "Being therefore justified by faith, we have peace with God through our Lord Jesus Christ." This same Jesus, who as "Crier" has gone before us, leads us into the arena. For Paul says, "Through whom also we have had our access by faith into this grace, . . ." i.e. access to the glorious arena, "wherein we stand." We have taken our position, in readiness for the fight, and "rejoice in the hope of the glory of God"—that is, in the prospect of wearing the crown with which the judge of the contest shall crown us.

A man who has thus taken his position in the arena is disappointed if there is no one to do battle with him. He

A STRENGTH OF THE SPIRIT

literally rejoices when an opponent appears with whom he may come to grips.

Therefore the apostle goes on to say, "And not only so," not only have we taken our stand in the arena, "but we rejoice in our tribulations." That is, we are glad to face an opponent; we would not be left standing in the center of the arena like fools, vainly waiting for someone to come. For to wrestle was our purpose! Because we know, so Paul concludes, "that tribulation worketh endurance, approvedness; and approvedness, hope; and hope putteth not to shame; because the love of God hath been shed abroad in our hearts through the Holy Spirit which was given unto us."

When we are attacked, when our opponent takes hold and attempts to throw us, only then does our strength appear. Then every muscle is strained; each fierce attack inspires more determined resistance; we exert ourselves to the utmost, putting forth all our strength to remain standing. And thus endurance is born.

When the first assailant slinks away, having failed to triumph over us, we have confidence to enter a second bout, and with an even stronger opponent. We have tested our strength; by enduring, we have proved our ability to endure. Thus *endurance worketh approvedness*. The tribulation of struggle called forth strength to endure; the endurance produced the confidence of approvedness; and with that new confidence hope waxes stronger—the hope of *never* being overcome by an assailant, the hope of eventually winning the crown.

Thus the child of God, struggling against the forces of evil in and around him, discovers within himself a God-given strength which enables him to *endure* all assault triumphantly.

V

Meekness

It is remarkable that patience, or endurance, is mentioned frequently in the New Testament and not in the Old. Surely, the recipients of God's grace under the Old Covenant also wrestled; theirs was a like holy faith with ours; they looked for the fulfilment of like promises of glory. Yet in reference to their spiritual life "patience" is never mentioned. Neither psalmist nor prophet exhorted them to patience or endurance. And when the New Testament makes mention of patience in the Old Testament, it is not in reference to an Israelite but to a man in Arabia, named Job. Patience (or endurance is not extolled in a Moses or an Elijah.

The reason for this lies in the difference between Old Testament and New Testament calling.

In Old Testament times, the people of God were a separate people, living apart from other nations, enclosed as it were within the limits of a special country. The church of the New Covenant, on the contrary, overflows the borders of nationality; it spreads to all people; it is in the midst of the world, and may not rest until the Cross of Christ has been planted to the very ends of the earth.

Consequently the faith of God's Old Testament people was subjected to tests quite different from those which try His New Testament children.

MEEKNESS

In Old Testament times, believers suffered oppression and scorn from those who were brothers according to the flesh; the followers of Jesus are subject to the scorn and vexations of the world.

Among brethren there was the kiss of a Judas, the oath of a Caiaphas who confessed the same God, and the mocking laugh of a Herod. But quite different is the enmity of the world—the coldness of a Pilate, who acquits and yet condemns, the mockery of rude Roman soldiers, the scourging and the crucifixion. Not as if there were no Judases in our ranks today, or as if there had been no enmity from the world in olden times. There are false brethren among us, and in olden times there were Pharaohs and Nebuchadnezzars. But the chief opposition to godliness in Israel came from false brethren, while among us the chief opposition is the antagonism of the world.

For these two diverse needs of His people, the Holy Spirit kindles two diverse virtues—overagainst hatred of false brethren *meekness;* overagainst the molestations of the world *endurance.*

That man is meek who resists the desire to return evil for evil, to retaliate with bitter words when he is wronged. That man has endurance who can stand firm and maintain his faith in God amid troubles and oppression.

Accordingly, in the Old Testament meekness is lauded; but in the New Testament endurance is enjoined.

Moses, the man of God, did not suffer from onslaughts of the world. His soul was constantly burdened with the complaints and murmurings of his own people. Therefore it is said of him, "Now the man Moses was very meek, above all men."

THE PRACTICE OF GODLINESS

And the Psalmist sings, "The meek shall inherit the earth" —words which Jesus quoted in His sermon on the Mount.

In the Old Testament the meek, though for a time downtrodden, were assured final triumph. "The Lord upholdeth the meek." "The meek will He guide in justice." "The meek shall eat and be satisfied." "He will beautify the meek with salvation." "The meek shall increase their joy in the Lord."

Job, on the other hand, is a glorious example of patience, or endurance. His suffering did not come from his own brethren but, under God's direction, from Satan. In one day he was bereft of his children and all his possessions. Then his body was afflicted with dreadful disease. In his trouble Job's great difficulty was not that he must conquer a desire for revenge, but that he must remain faithful to his God in spite of crushing adversities and in the face of taunts. Job's triumph was not that he remained meek overagainst his wife and his friends, but that he permitted no one and nothing to shake his faith in God.

The Israelites, too, had to wrestle "to keep the faith." That is evident from their history and also from the Psalms. But in the main their enemies, the Assyrians, the Babylonians, did not demand that they forswear God and worship idols. Except once—and that one attempt called forth a miracle which caused the great Nebuchadnezzar to humble himself before the God of heaven.

However insistent one may be upon the one-ness of Old Testament and New Testament faith, nevertheless there is a great difference. Theirs was a time of shadows and promises. They had only the assurances; we have, at least in part, the reality. They awaited the coming of the Messiah; they longed for His salvation and while waiting they sought shelter in

MEEKNESS

the secret place of the Most High. They found refuge in His tabernacles while the promised glory tarried, and they constantly spurred one another on, as we read in the Psalms, to renewed trust in the faithfulness of Him who promised. "Wait for the Lord, O my soul." "For Thee, O Lord, do I wait all the day."

For the New Testament believer the wonders of the manger and the cross are realities. True, he awaits the return of the Lord. And he is also called to meekness, particularly in relation to his fellow-believers. But meekness and waiting are not his chief concern. He has a battle to fight, a God-given calling to go out into the world, where he will meet resistance, where enemies will try to destroy him body and soul. Against these he must have strength to stand, he needs the spiritual strength to *endure*.

Jesus, who suffered much of the priests and scribes, speaks of his own meekness, but never of endurance. "Learn of me that I am meek and lowly of heart." "Behold, your King cometh, meek . . . ." And He a King! His apostles praise ". . . the meekness and gentleness of Christ . . ." (II Cor. 10:1) toward the people of Israel and their blind leaders. But they also praise His endurance, His steadfastness or patience, before Pilate and throughout His suffering upon the cross (II Thess. 3:5).

VI

The Man of Sorrows

ENDURANCE is a Christian virtue in a very special sense. Not as we commonly understand "Christian virtue"—merely a virtue commanded and exemplified by Christ. But a *Christian* virtue because it is inseparably linked with Christ. Endurance originated with the coming of Jesus into the world; wherever it is found in a Christian it is his through Christ; and with the return of Christ there shall no longer be need of it.

In his original state, man did not require endurance. The command was, "Do this and thou shalt live." Adam and Eve in Paradise were under the "covenant of works," as our forefathers called it. Man was made for the joy of eternal life with God, but he had to earn it. It was not to be his as a gift of grace, "without money and without price." That glorious gospel was not one of the glories of Paradise. Man was to attain eternal life by his own strength; it was to be a reward of merit.

Note the contrast. For Adam, strength preceded the possession of eternal life; under the Covenant of Works, he was *given* strength to *do, after* which he would be rewarded with eternal life. And that reward none would try to take from him. But under the Covenant of Grace eternal life is *first given* to man, and with that gift the strength to keep it, while at the same time there is an equal power, the power of evil, which strives to wrest the gift from us.

THE MAN OF SORROWS

God brought His Christ into the world to redeem sinners. And had there been no sin, Christ would not have been sent.

At first the coming of the Christ into the world was only in *spoken word;* there was prophecy to utter that word; there was altar service to symbolize the meaning of the word; there was a people in whom this word lived; there was a history which gradually unrolled the word into deed; and there was a separateness which prevented that the word should be lost or forgotten.

In opposition to this spoken word Satan hardly showed himself. He struck his first blow in Paradise, but that was before the Covenant of Grace. He played his part with Job, but that was outside of Israel. He is mentioned in Psalm 109, and again at the time of David's numbering of the people. Zacharias mentions him in prophecy. But he is not at all prominent in the life of Israel.

It is in the wilderness of Judea that he steps forth boldly at last to face the Word become Flesh, the Son of God. Then the Prince of demons takes up his position against the Prince of the Lord's hosts.

For then at last the spoken and symbolized word was visible. Then there was Holiness upon earth in such form that it could be resisted and opposed, it could be besmirched and perhaps destroyed.

But against the attacks of Satan, Christ was adamant. All Satan's frenzy and hatred were vain. He did not win even a momentary victory.

That heavenly strength which overcame every effort to thrust the Holy One out of the world is endurance. Christ was the first to display endurance overagainst Satan. He was truly the patient one.

THE PRACTICE OF GODLINESS

And it is He who works that same strength in those who are His.

This patience of Jesus is not displayed in His attitude toward His people, who grieved Him and persecuted Him, but in His spiritual struggles against Satan. First in the wilderness, later during His physical suffering in Pilate's jugdment hall and upon the cross, He was steadfast, He endured.

Satan left nothing untried in his efforts to crush that glorious, holy, divine life, to corrupt it, to destroy it. But the holiness of Jesus was neither marred nor even slightly soiled. The Father caused Him to walk as it were through fire, but it did not singe His robes or His hair; He plunged Him like white wool into sticky mire, but the whiteness came out resplendent. The full glory of Jesus' endurance is revealed when, on the third morning, He arises from the grave; He endured that last enemy, and overcame it—death!

Thus ended Satan's battle over the Word *as such.* There is nothing more he can do now against the Christ.

But there is another warfare, another opportunity for Satan. He can still fight those who confess the Son, the followers of the Christ.

Jesus ascended into heaven. To those whom He left behind He entrusted the great cause of carrying the torch of God. From the Sun of Righteousness sparks were kindled in thousands of hearts. Toward these followers of Christ Satan now directs his hatred, a hatred made even more terrible, if possible, by the humiliating defeat. And the followers of Christ are weaker than their Master. So with renewed fury Satan returns to the attack.

THE MAN OF SORROWS

Hence the persecutions of the early Christians. Hence the spiritual agonies, worse than physical pain, which the followers of Christ experience.

Satan has never ceased in his efforts to tear the truth from the grasp of God's children, and to wrench them from the hand of God. But against his attacks the followers of Jesus have triumphed, throughout the centuries, by *endurance*.

They have not yielded. They have not swerved from the path. They have not lost hold of that which they once received. Even when they died in the flames, the spark of life spurted from them into other hearts, and thousands were converted that they might carry on.

The martyrs *endured*. By the *patience* of the saints Satan's plans were frustrated.

Whence that struggle to endure? Was it of ourselves?

No, my dear reader!

But what appeared to be, was not. Christ had ascended to heaven. Yet He was *not* gone. On the contrary, having taken our flesh with him into heaven, he established once and for all His power over the world and over the spirits that hover destructively about it.

Jesus and His own—they are not two but *one*. Even as the branches are one with the vine.

Most surely *they* would have retreated, stumbled, succumbed. But He, dwelling within them, cannot be conquered. His strength was greater than their weakness.

When Satan thought he had only his one-time friends to wrestle with, he found himself once again fighting a losing battle with the Lion of Judah!

In Him is our *endurance*.

Therefore it does not fail.

VII

Maranatha

PATIENCE, or endurance, flows forth from Jesus; it ought to accompany confession of Him; it glorifies Him; it is inseparable from His service.

There is a story told of an altar boy who, in the fulfillment of his duties, was called upon to hold a fragrant incense burner before the great king Alexander. While he was thus holding the censer, a live coal burst out and fell upon the boy's naked arm. But the boy did not flinch. Though he could smell the odor of his own burning flesh, he held the censer steady before the king. How could he permit his pain to interrupt a service in honor of a king's majesty.

You who are the Lord's, such is your calling in the service of Jesus, your Lord.

Your life is to be one continuous flow of praise, one constant faithful service. Should Satan in some manner press a live coal into your flesh, hoping to cause you to drop the censer of your love and worship, you must not waver; though the fire scorch you, you must keep your arm steadily outstretched, to the honor of your Lord.

Whatever may come, though the waves go over your head, you may not retreat nor waver. "Keep what thou hast!" is the watchword of the Christian. The apostle exclaims triumphantly, "I have *kept* the faith; henceforth there is laid up for me a crown of righteousness!"

MARANATHA

The "keeping," the *not losing hold of*, that is the endurance of the child of God.

All oppression, all scorn, all persecution has no other purpose than to induce the Christian to give up his most precious possession, to let go his faith, to lose his hope.

But he does not let go. He holds his treasure in a grasp that will not loosen, and he wears out the enemy with the unshakable strength of endurance.

"O Timothy," Paul cries out to his faithful helper, "*keep that which is committed to thy trust!*" Nothing else matters, says the writer to the Hebrews, "if we but *hold fast* our confidence and the joy of our hope firm to the end." Elsewhere we read, "Let us *hold fast* the confession of our hope, that it waver not!" And when Satan, seeing he cannot wrest our precious possession from us, attempts to drag us down bodily, then we must, like Moses, endure "as seeing Him who is invisible," by faith.

For endurance and *faith* go hand in hand, as Paul writes to the Thessalonians. "We glory in you in the churches of God for your patience *and faith* in all your persecutions and afflictions." (Compare Rev. 2:19, and 13:10). Endurance consists of just that, a holding on to our *faith* in spite of suffering or scorn, not permitting trouble to darken the truth of God, always ready when asked, "Do you still hold fast to your righteousness?" to answer unhesitatingly, "Yes!"

Endurance is also linked with *love*. Paul writes to the persecuted Thessalonians, "The Lord direct your hearts into the love of God and into the patience (endurance) of Christ." Perhaps you at times discover secret rebellion deep within your heart even while you apparently resign yourself to suffering. That would indicate a doubt of the love of God. Satan plants such seeds of doubt within the heart, and thus chills your love for the Christ. All things work together for good. But only "to them that love God," to those whose love for God is not sapped by pain and trouble. Indeed, the secret of true endurance is love, love which sustains the weak, which gives strength to the broken reed against the stormy winds of trial.

Then, too, by our endurance we retain that other of the three beautiful jewels—*hope*. Paul writes to the Romans, "That through patience (endurance) and through the comfort of the scriptures we might have hope." That hope is a window through which we catch glimpses of eternal glory. Satan desires to shut off our view with the heavy curtains of doubt and trouble. But he cannot. With the strength of endurance we who are Christ's push aside the curtains and once more gaze upon the glories to come.

For even as endurance originates in Jesus, it also finds its fulfilment in the Beloved One. If there were no sure *hope of Jesus' return*, there would be no strength to endure.

A Christian faith which finds its end in the manger and the cross, and which has no longing for the return of the Lord, is neither healthy nor apostolic nor true. Jesus' coming to the manger and to the cross is inseparable from His coming again upon the clouds. The latter is necessary to complete the former. If Jesus were not coming again, the Divine drama would be without a closing scene, without the unfolding of the plot and the solution of the mystery.

A Christian is not the irrational dreamer he is often thought to be, with impossible aspirations and unattainable ideals. He knows very well that he was created not for suffering but for happiness. He is fully aware that suffering is unnatural and that joy should be man's portion. In the depths of his soul he is convinced that man can willingly

MARANATHA

suffer the miseries of the moment only if he is certain that, in due time, they will be followed by joy and happiness.

He knows, too, that it is pleasanter to be "clothed in soft raiment and live in kings' palaces" than to wear camel's hair and roam the wilderness or hide in dens and holes. But he knows even more surely that there is no comparison between transient earthly pleasures and the immeasurable glory and beauty of the eternal Jerusalem.

Very soberly, therefore, he makes his choice. On one side of the scales are the joys and riches of this world. On the other side are the thorns and the cross, side by side with the glories of eternal life. The Christian sees clearly that one side of the scale wholly outweighs the other. His conclusion is, 'Yes, I count all things but loss, but refuse, for the excellency of the knowledge of Christ Jesus my Lord." And to others he expresses his conviction triumphantly. "My brother, my sister, no matter how intense the suffering of this present time may be, it is not to be compared with the glory that shall be!" That shall be—not this side of heaven without God, but in heaven and with Him who is the Fountain of all good, the glorious and eternal Son of God. Shall be—when He returns!

VIII

Cross Bearing

IF we think that the earthly pathway of God's children is for the most part pleasant and easy, with only an occasional cross, we are mistaken. The child of God who is new upon the way, and weathers his first storm, may think: This will soon be over and then the breezes will blow gently again. But as we go on, we learn by many a disappointment, as well as from the Word of the Lord, that such is not our lot. When one wave of the sea breaks, another follows close behind. So troubles continually roll over the heads of God's children. The cross must be carried daily.

"All who would live a godly life shall suffer persecution." And "without much tribulation ye shall not enter into the Kingdom of God." Never can we escape the cross. And the proof of the genuineness of our endurance is just this, that we take up our cross daily, taking such burdens as God lays upon us, and bear the cross upon the way where He leads.

Only the child of God, he who is saved by the blood of the Son of God, is a cross bearer. For only such suffering may be counted cross-bearing which is borne for love of God, in the strength of Christ, and for His Name's sake. None other deserves that title.

The Christian's sorrows and burdens are not always obvious. The cross is not always one which the world can see. Indeed not. Bitterest of all the agonies which wring the human heart are often those that only God knows.

CROSS BEARING

What, then, composes the cross?

The cross consists not of those things which oppose *you*, but of those things which oppose *your faith*. Whatever threatens, weakens, or undermines your faith, or interferes with its activity, is your cross.

It may be a weakness of the body; it may be a thorn in the flesh. It may also be the scorn you bear because of the church of God. It may be the miscarriage of plans you thought were very good, and the frustration of your highest hopes. Assuredly, it also includes the sins which beset you from without, from fellow-men. And, worst of all, the sins which dwell within your own heart, which pain you and trouble you.

For we must remember that, if the sins of others try our patience, the sins within our own hearts are even harder to bear. Yet we are called to endurance also in regard to them. Do not misunderstand — this does not and never can mean that you must let your sin have its way. Endurance is a holding fast to faith, whatever may come. And our own sins are a part of that "whatever." Over against one's sin endurance means that, though I prick and burn my fingers on it, I shall not let it shake my faith.

And that is the heaviest and bitterest burden.

For we are so prone to become impatient with that dreadful weed within the heart. How firmly we have resolved to root it out! We've tugged at it, passionately determined to cast it into the depths of hell. But in vain. It's still there. It pricks us again and its poison gets under our skin once more. We have prayed, so often and so fervently, that God would take it away. But He does not! And we cry, "Why not?" Then we become impatient. In our impatience we tug

THE PRACTICE OF GODLINESS

at the weed again, only to tear our hands on its thorns once more. And our steadfastness wavers.

We ought not to deal with it thus.

God's blessing does not rest upon such striving against the sins of the flesh.

When we were reborn of the Spirit, God saw fit to leave that thorny weed in our hearts. We cannot understand why. We cannot fathom the wisdom of God. But we must acknowledge it. And therefore we may not lose patience with this which He has deemed best for us. We are to endure it. And thus it will serve to drive us to Him the more often, that we may learn from Him how to avoid the thorns and the poison.

That weed will be there until you are called to glory. Then you shall lay down your earthly tabernacle, and with it at last be rid of all the thorns of sin.

But meanwhile God does not intend that it shall hurt you. On the contrary, it should bring you to a state of quietness before Him. You will learn to be careful lest you hurt yourself on the thorns, and you thus will learn to temper your impatience and curb your unhallowed restlessness. That weed will drive you to God, where you must learn patience, where you will find the calmness of endurance.

So the cross is multiform.

And for the bearing of this multiform cross there is abundant strength, even strength to triumph.

Flesh and blood protest against cross bearing and resent it. Human sinful nature cannot willingly bear such burdens. It is only by the gracious operation of the Holy Spirit that the Christian learns to take up his cross with eagerness, and at last even to glory in it.

* * *

CROSS BEARING

But if you should take the attitude: I must be strong to bear this my cross; it will require all the effort I can muster: I shall exert myself and gradually develop the strength to endure — then, do believe it, then you are in a bad way. For then one of two results will ensue. Either the Lord will cause your self-dependent efforts to fail (which is by far preferable), or He will permit you to develop a sickly strength of your own by means of your own miserable efforts; and that will prove to be poison to your soul.

No, it must not be thus. I must not only admit, but also fully realize, that to bear the cross steadfastly day after day, to bear it when it tears my flesh and heart, to bear it as Jesus would have me bear it, is beyond my strength and endurance. Lord, thy servant cannot! Who among those born in sin is able to perform so gigantic a task?

If this is your sincere confession, if your inner heart thus truly feels its helplessness, then through prayer your "I cannot!" becomes "I can!" For he who feels utterly helpless seeks shelter in the Almighty. And never has anyone sought comfort with Jesus but that he was also given strength to endure.

Then you will not understand your own willingness to bear a cross against which your very nature protests. Your own flesh whispers, "Cast it off!" Friends around you say, "You cannot bear it!" Satan taunts, "You'll have to give it up!" But you hold your head high and you do *not* cast it off.

Even though you may be nailed to the cross and men cry out, "If you are free in Christ, come down!" you remain steadfast. You endure unto death, unto the grave; not in your own strength but in the strength of your Lord.

This then is your endurance, that through all trials and temptations you *keep the faith;* you are *upheld by faith;*

when the way is difficult and wearisome, you are found walking in the path of God's will *by faith.*

If your wrestling is sincere, if cross-bearing is to you a serious matter, then Satan will place many a stumbling block in your way and bring about many a fall. That is to be expected. But no matter how often we fall, or how long the evil one may hold us down, we do again wrestle free and regain our feet. Though weary and well-nigh exhausted, we do not give up until the enemy slinks away in defeat once more.

Endurance does not imply that you never for a moment lose faith. It does imply that every struggle ends with the outcry, "More than conquerors through Jesus Christ who giveth me strength!"

Patience, then, is not submission but the exercise of strength. It is not indifference to, but keen awareness of suffering. It is the strength whereby we never let go but ever hold fast to that which was given us by God's grace. Patience is that virtue granted God's children, whereby Christ enables us to endure the cross, while we look for His coming again.

PART III

HUMILITY BEFORE GOD

.

"Worshipping with fasting and supplications."
         LUKE 2:37.

I

God's Word Our Guide

THERE is a fasting ordained of God. Such fasting has been practised by the people of God throughout all history.

In the early centuries of Christianity it remained pure. Later it degenerated; its meaning and essence were distorted until it was little more than a superstitious rite.

But in the sixteenth century, along with all the other reforms, fasting regained its true place. Then, for a time. it was commonly practised among Christians of the Reformation.

Today there are still some found among the godly who fast. But very few. The practice has gradually died out.

We no longer have congregational fasting. We have become estranged from fasting, and we do not count it among the means of edification. Our leaders seldom if ever suggest or recommend it. And what our fathers thought of it is not even known among us. In fact, the very mention of fasting suggests Roman Catholicism.

That is why we wish to bring before you the teaching of God's Word in regard to fasting — fasting as our fathers taught and practised it, and as it applies to us.

Do not let the desires of the flesh turn you away from these our earnest words. It is so easy to label "superstition" anything that thwarts those desires!

THE PRACTICE OF GODLINESS

But, as Calvin says, "Let us talk a bit about fasting, since many believe it is quite unnecessary, failing to appreciate the benefits they may derive from it; some have discarded it entirely, as if it had no value; and if we do not use it rightly, we may easily fall into superstition."

In our day very nearly all of us have the opinion which "some" held in Calvin's day — that fasting is quite unnecessary. And most of us have discarded it entirely.

Yet in these times of spiritual poverty not one means of grace or one channel of closer fellowship with God should be neglected.

Therefore Christendom should return to fasting.

Not because Calvin taught it. But because he taught it on the basis of God's Word.

* * *

God's Word is our guide.

For some, orthodoxy consists in seeking out passages in the Word to support their own opinions. At the same time they probably hold to other ideas which are contrary to the Word, and they ignore that with which they do not agree.

That is a perverted approach to the Word of God.

For the Word of God and human ideas are in opposition to each other. God's Word gives us a view of the world and of man and man's soul that is quite different from the purely human opinion.

Nevertheless there are many, ministers as well as laymen, who view man and his problems from the viewpoint of the world. They know no other anthropology or psychology than that of the world's scientific thinkers, and they build

GOD'S WORD OUR GUIDE

a system of religious thought upon ground which differs from the Word. Their foundation is not Scripture, but human insight.

For the Christian, God's Word is source-book. He bases his thoughts and opinions upon that Word.

Even so we may err. But at least our starting point is valid. While if we seek to support our own pre-conceived ideas from Scripture we reverse the divine order.

God's majesty and sovereignty require that we believe God's Word not because of what it says, but because *it is His Word* Not because we think it beautiful and true, but because *He has spoken it.*

Now in regard to fasting...

The question before us is not whether we shall profit from fasting; or whether there is danger of its becoming a superstitious practice; nor whether our leaders approve of it.

But only: *Is it Scriptural?*

We may put it thus: Does God speak of fasting in His Word? And if so, how does He evaluate it?

Does He disapprove? Does He speak of fasting as harmful to spiritual life and as something to be avoided?

Then our church fathers who recommended it were in error.

Or is the Word of God indifferent to fasting, speaking of it as a harmless but worthless custom?

Then the subject is not important enough to discuss. It does not touch our consciences.

Or does God speak of it as praiseworthy, as emanating from true spiritual life, as appropriate to His worship and befitting godliness, and of value to those who seek God?

Then our church fathers were right and we are in error; then it is the duty of the child of God to restore fasting to its proper place of honor.

* * *

Before continuing, let us make clear that by fasting we do not mean mere temperance or moderation, but actual abstinence from food for a longer or shorter period.

Temperance and moderation are required of a Christian always. Intemperance is sin.

Fasting, however, is occasional. Nature itself forbids continual fasting. It must be an exception, not a rule.

We would then define fasting as: *a temporary abstaining from customary food or drink, for devotional reasons.*

To quote Calvin once more, "That we err not, let us describe fasting. We do not understand it to mean merely a frugal partaking of food. For the life of godliness is always temperate and sober. But there is besides that a temporary withdrawal from our usual manner of living, perhaps for a day, or for a period, when we allow ourselves less food and drink than usual — less in amount, in quality, and in frequency."

What, then, does the Word of God teach concerning such fasting?

II

Biblical Fasting

FIRST of all let us note three significant passages of Scripture: Exodus 34, I Kings 19, and Matthew 4.

There we read of three men, each of whom passed through a remarkable forty-day fast. These were the three who appeared to the disciples in glory upon Mount Tabor; these were the three through whom God revealed Himself preeminently.

We read of our Saviour that *when he had fasted forty days,* he hungered.

Elijah, having been fed by the angel, *"went in the strength of that meat forty days and forty nights* unto Mount Horeb, the mount of God."

And Moses, when he was upon the mount with the Lord forty days and forty nights, "did neither eat bread nor drink water." As he himself relates it. "When I was gone up into the mount to receive the tables of stone, even the tables of the covenant which the Lord made with you, then I abode in the mount *forty days and forty nights, I neither did eat bread nor drink water."*

These fastings were very exceptional. We are most surely not called upon to emulate such a fast of nearly *six* weeks. It would require miraculous intervention, and nowhere in Scripture are we led to expect such a wonder to be wrought upon us.

THE PRACTICE OF GODLINESS

But there was special significance in this fasting, closely related to the spiritual struggle through which each had to wrestle in the Name of the Lord. For each it was a momentous experience — not a superstitious vagary, but a deed in which the Name of God was honored and glorified. Moses fasted in the presence of God upon the mount; Elijah was sustained by food which the angel of the Lord brought him; and Jesus, when He was about to fast, was led into the wilderness by the Holy Spirit. For each, the mysterious experience had a deep spiritual meaning.

Note in the second place that Jesus frequently spoke of fasting with approval. In the Sermon on the Mount, He placed prayer and alms-giving and fasting on a level. When warning against the misuse of fasting, he prescribed how it ought to be done. "And when you fast, anoint thy head and wash thy face, that thou be not seen of men to fast, but of thy Father who is in secret; and thy Father who seeth in secret shall recompense thee."

Jesus thus, in the third place, plainly and explicitly declared fasting to be an act of faith which God would in His grace reward. In Matthew 6:18 he says, "When you fast, do so without outward show, for your father who is in secret and who seeth in secret *shall reward you*."

Jesus also recommended fasting as the one effective weapon in certain struggles against Satan when He said. "This kind goeth not out but by fasting and prayer" (Matt. 17:21).

Finally, Jesus said of His disciples that though they did not fast while He was with them, afterwards they would do so. "Can ye make the children of the bride-chamber fast while the bridegroom is with them? But the days will come when the bridegroom shall be taken away from them, and *then shall they fast in those days*" (Luke 5,34, 35). Thus

BIBLICAL FASTING

He predicted that there would be fasting among His people after His departure.

In the early church, according to the writings of the apostles, this prophecy was verified. There was frequent fasting. The short record of Acts tells of no less than three occasions, all spoken of favorably, all characterized by sincere godliness.

It was while men were *fasting and praying* that the Holy Spirit gave special revelation of His will concerning Paul and Barnabas. Acts 13:2: "And as they ministered to the Lord *and fasted*, the Holy Spirit said, Separate me Barnabas and Saul..."

Then, to understand further the meaning of the Spirit, they besought the Lord again in prayer and fasting. "And when they had fasted and prayed, and laid their hands on them, they sent them away."

From Acts 14:23 it is evident that under Paul's direction prayer and fasting accompanied the appointment of elders. "And when they had appointed for them elders in every church, and had prayed with fasting, they commended them to the Lord on whom they had believed."

Paul also taught by precept. Writing to the Corinthians he says, "That ye may give yourselves to fasting and prayer" (I Cor. 7:5). He cites himself as example, "... commending ourselves as ministers of God, in much paticence ... in watchings, in fastings" (II Cor. 6:5) and (II Cor. 11:27) he tells how he was "in labor, in fasting often, in cold and nakedness."

In Old Testament times the prophets frequently exhorted the people to fasting in the Name of the Lord. "Therefore also now, *saith the Lord,* turn ye even to me with all your heart, and *with fasting* and with weeping and with mourning, and rend your heart and not your garments, and turn unto the Lord your God, for He is gracious and merciful..." (Joel 2:12).

In Jeremiah 36:9 we read, "They proclaimed a fast before the Lord to all the people in Jerusalem," at the express direction of the prophet.

The prophets themselves resorted to fasting. Daniel says, "And I set my face unto the Lord God, to seek by prayer and supplication, with fasting, and sackcloth and ashes" (Daniel 9:3).

Old Testament fastings were not proclaimed in times of prosperity nor in times of murmuring and discontent, but in times of distress, when the soul was humbled before God. And such supplication and fasting was frequently followed by answered prayer and blessing.

Ezra (chapter 8:21) writes, "Then I proclaimed a fast, that we might afflict ourselves before our God, to seek of him a right way for us, and for our little ones, and for all our substances... So we fasted and besought our God for this, and he was intreated of us."

* * *

Having thus summarized the teaching of Scripture in regard to fasting, can we have any doubt as to its spiritual value? Can we doubt whether it is a godly practice, and according to God's will?

In the Middle Ages, fasting had degenerated into a mere ritual imposed by man. But the Reformers, freeing it from the encumbrance of human rules, renewed the practice in accordance with the requirements of Scripture, that it might be well-pleasing unto God. They recommended it as an

BIBLICAL FASTING

expression of godly living. Luther and Calvin and other Reformers proclaimed general fasting in times of trouble and when evil threatened the church, and also when a minister was called or some problem of the congregation must be solved. To them a day of *prayer* was a day of prayer and fasting.

Today fasting is a rarity. Few ever think of it. Few remember seeing mother or father fast. Even in times of distress we fail to take recourse to fasting and prayer, as did our forefathers.

When, in the early days of the Reformation, there was trouble among Christian brothers, communion was suspended and a day of fasting and prayer was proclaimed, that men might humble themselves before God and be reconciled to each other.

Now we reason and argue, and strive to lay the blame on one or another, and too often we go our way, even to the Table of the Lord, unreconciled.

Is ours a period of greater spirituality? Can we afford to dispense with a means of godliness of which our fathers felt a need?

THE PRACTICE OF GODLINESS

III

Godliness

FASTING is but a more emphatic expression of Paul's outcry, "Wretched man that I am! Who will deliver me from this body of death?"

For it is the body that protests when we would fast. It is the body that occupies almost all of our time, demanding to be fed and clothed and tended. We are so busy from morning till night fulfilling the demands of the body, that there is barely a half hour left in the day for quiet meditation and prayer. That is a common complaint.

Paul says, "I buffet my body and bring it into bondage..." Thereby he reverses the natural tendency which says, "My body is master and I am its servant."

It is amazing how the physical often dominates, even in a Christian home. A large proportion of time is spent in the procuring, preparing and eating of food, in cleaning, sewing, mending, buying and beautifying. And above all, how largely our minds—our conversations, plans and wishes—are occupied with these things!

Would Paul's words be a fitting motto on our walls: "I bring my body into bondage"?

Not only does the physical occupy a great share of our time. There is the further danger that it may actually dominate the spiritual. Particularly when men abandon themselves to the enjoyment of food and drink.

GODLINESS

Our meals should be festive events in the home life, an expression of family unity, an enjoyment of each other's company even more than of the food.

But the over-indulgence sometimes practised, especially on feast days, makes one wonder if the body is truly the temple of the Holy Spirit—even though a blessing is asked at the beginning of the meal, and the Bible appears at the end.

When the mind and heart are so largely occupied with earthly affairs and with the enjoyment of food, drink and clothing, does prayer flow spontaneously?

Ah no, we are not advocating that godliness consists of "touch not, taste not" rules. Nor can moderation in food and drink take the place of faith and hope and love. There is nothing more repugnant to us than a piety which tends toward outward show.

Our intention is quite the opposite. We would have you *know* yourself, know if perhaps the service of external things is a hindrance in your prayer life, if it does not chill your love and prevent close fellowship with your Lord.

To counteract this danger, can there be a more natural remedy than fasting?

In many of our Christian homes Sunday is still observed with impressive quietness and solemnity. There is a hush in the home. No running up and down the stairs, no rushing about. But a subdued, restful spirit of solemnity. In the kitchen, too, there is little activity, for the meals are of the simplest, merely enough to satisfy hunger.

Much like such a Lord's Day, carried a bit farther, were the prayer and fast days of our fore-fathers. Sobriety in food

and clothing, a minimum of work, and a conscious subduing of the spirit before God.

Total abstinence from food was suggested, but not required. A bit of bread or a drink of milk might prevent the distraction of physical discomfort. The strong made no rules for the weak; little children were given enough to content them. There was complete freedom, combined with the sincere desire to subdue the demands of the body in order that the spirit might the better worship God.

Appearance, too, expressed humility before God. Not by obvious dishabille, or by pharisaical sadness of face, but simply by abstaining from the self-satisfaction of ornament.

As far as possible, daily tasks were laid aside. The entire congregation spent as much as possible of the day in church, gathering in quiet groups between services to discuss spiritual matters, as in the presence of the Lord. It was a day of congregational mourning and prayer.

Fasting as a family was slightly different. The occasion was perhaps some adversity, or a spirit of disharmony in the home, or perhaps some special sin of a member of the family. The father, as head of the house, would then enjoin a day of fasting—not as punishment, but as a "humbling before God." And the end of such a day usually saw peace and contentment restored, while the spirit of prayer lingered for many a day afterward.

Then there was also perpetual fasting. As one who is bowed in mourning cannot eat, so one oppressed with spiritual sorrow may refuse food for a day. An overwhelming sense of having grieved the Lord, and a longing for renewed peace with God, these sentiments were not uncommon in those days. And they caused men to humble themselves in fasting before Him who searches the hearts.

GODLINESS

We seldom hear of such fasting today.

We have become estranged from it. Men shrug their shoulders and smile at the mention of it. In our thoughts it is associated only with Roman Catholicism.

Physical hygiene has a place of importance in our lives. But spiritual hygiene? That hardly seems worth the effort.

Good behaviour, decency and good manners, even these are almost too much to expect.

And where is the genuine thirst for fellowship with the eternal God?

We are not referring to unbelievers. They have their vain ideals. We have in mind confessors of the Name of Christ. And we would ask: What is it that motivates your life? What is most important to you? Is it how you may remain in sweet fellowship with the Lord? Enjoy His presence? And know the peace of reconciliation with Him?

Is that what motivates you and guides your steps? Is that your reason for choosing what to do or not to do?

If not, is your spiritual life what it ought to be?

Mere abstinence from food is not pleasing to God.

But when it is motivated by true humility before God, it is a means of regaining blessed fellowship with Him.

IV

Not by Bread Alone

UNHESITATINGLY we recommend fasting for the Christians of today. In fact, we are inclined to say that there is more reason for fasting in our day than ever before. Corrupted human nature yearns for luxury, and tends to become more corrupt as wealth and luxury increase. God knows that we cannot well be checked except by burdens and sorrows. And He himself has suggested fasting, by means of which we may guard against the unspiritual influence of ease and luxury.

Israel's experience in the wilderness contains a lesson to which we may well give heed.

When Jesus thrust away the temptation of Satan, he quoted from Deuteronomy 8, "Man shall not live by bread alone, but by every word that proceedeth out of the mouth of God."

These were Moses' words, spoken in reference to the forty years' wandering in the wilderness. And Moses tells us the reason for that prolonged hardship, "The Lord your God led thee these forty years in the wilderness to humble thee, . . . to prove thee, to know what was in thine heart. . . . He humbled thee and suffered thee to hunger . . . to do thee good at thy latter end. That your heart should not say, 'My power and the might of mine hand hath gotten me this wealth,' but that thou shalt remember the Lord thy God; for

NOT BY BREAD ALONE

it is he that giveth thee power to get wealth, that he may establish his covenant which he sware unto thy fathers, as it is this day."

In Old Testament times "to humble one's soul" meant the same as "to fast." Moses suggests this also in the words, "He humbled thee and suffered thee to hunger."

Why did God cause His people to hunger? To teach them that they were dependent upon Him from moment to moment. To teach them that "man doth not live by bread only, but by whatever proceeds from the mouth of God."

These words must not be interpreted as contrasting food for the body and food for the soul. They do not at all mean: Your soul must be fed as well as your body.

In the Hebrew, "every word that proceedeth from the mouth of God means "all things, all power, *whatsoever* cometh from the mouth of God." And here it signifies the Manna, which came directly from the mouth of God, from the Word of His power.

When Israel had bread which they themselves prepared from their own meal and in their own ovens, they could say, "My strength and my hands have obtained this food."

But Manna took away all opportunity for such self-exaltation. They *found* Manna, found it lying on the ground, ready to eat, sent by God's creative word, and they found it according to individual need. as Moses explicitly stated.

Paul calls it "spiritual food." Asaph, in Psalm 78, sings of "the bread of angels." And our Lord taught us that the Manna was a symbol of His redemptive work when He said, "Your fathers ate Manna in the wilderness; I am the living bread come down from heaven, that a man may eat thereof and not die."

THE PRACTICE OF GODLINESS

And does not the Manna in the wilderness remind us of Paradise, where man also ate freely from the bountiful hand of God?

But man was not satisfied with the abundance of Paradise. He was not content to live thus in entire reliance upon God. He deliberately put forth his hand to take also the one fruit God had forbidden.

Consequently in the punishment which followed, man who would not live *from the hand of God* was bidden to "eat bread in the sweat of his face."

But the punishment, far from humbling man, has inspired him to a pride of independence. By his own labor, or by making others labor for him, he acquires abundance. And seated at his groaning board he boasts, "All this have I acquired by my strength and ingenuity."

In subsequent history, food and the desire for food played a striking part.

All mankind fell into the sin of independence and pride. "They were eating and drinking . . . until the day that Noah entered into the ark and the flood came."

After the flood, the same evil tendency was soon evident again. Noah planted the vine and was the first to succumb to the intoxication of wine.

Later God separated Himself a people. Abraham received the sacramental sign of bread and wine from Melchizedek.

Famine drove first Abraham, later Isaac, and also Jacob to Egypt. They looked to the full barns of Egypt for help, not yet knowing that there is life in the power of God's Word.

Because of food, Abraham had trouble over Sarah, Isaac came into difficulty about Rebekah, Jacob and all Israel became bondslaves.

NOT BY BREAD ALONE

Hunger brought about Esau's fall. He sold his birthright for a mess of pottage.

Isaac's desire for tasty food was the occasion of deception which resulted in family tragedy.

The early history of Israel is clouded by the need of food and the lack of higher knowledge.

When the sons of Jacob were offered the beautiful land of Goshen, they committed much the same sin as Esau, *preferring the plenty of Egypt to the promised land.*

Their motto should have been:

> *His mighty arm upholds His own*
> *And guards their souls from death.*

But they were unfaithful. And they paid the awful penalty of having to throw their babes into the Nile, and of serving in abject slavery.

All this history throws light upon the meaning of the Manna which God provided in the wilderness.

In the first place, the chosen people had to pass through the same test which had been laid upon Adam. They must live by faith, live from the hand of God.

"He caused thee to hunger to prove thee, to know what was in thine heart, whether thou wouldest keep his commandments or no."

And secondly, they must die to the sin which had brought them to Egypt. Hunger, need of food, had enticed them from Canaan. Now they were encamped at the door of Egypt without food, in order that their hearts might be tested. Would the desire for food draw them back to Egypt? Or, having learned their lesson, would they look to heaven now?

The Israelites failed, as did Adam. They longed for Egypt.

The enormity of their sin is not clear to us except by thus tracing their history. Their hankering after the fleshpots of Egypt was a disobedience. a disloyalty, a lack of faith—with special significance.

It became evident that Israel could not save itself, that there is salvation only in Him who should come, who would also be *tempted by hunger in the wilderness;* but who, withstanding the temptation, would be victorious where Adam fell and Israel failed.

SEEK YE FIRST

V

Seek Ye First . . .

THE mystery of contentment lies in childlike faith *that God cares for us.*
Anxiety is then superfluous, if not *sinful.*

Our children set us an example of such faith. They are busy at school or at play, without thought of preparing meals or earning a living. Father and Mother take care of that! When dinner time arrives, the children take their places at the table fully confident that there will be food.

They know food can be withheld as punishment; yet when they sit down to eat they do not look upon food as a reward for service. They are members of the family, and each must simply do what he ought to do, in his or her particular position. That is all. Their needs *are supplied.*

This golden rule of life Jesus applies to those whom He has redeemed. They are not to be servants, working for reward; they are to have the freedom of children.

The good people of Galilee, too, worked in the sweat of their faces. Enjoyment of today's food was spoiled by worry about tomorrow's. "What shall we eat tomorrow? What shall we drink, and wherewith shall we clothe ourselves tomorrow?"

Jesus disapproves. "That is after the manner of the heathen," he tells them. "It does not befit a child of God. You have a Father in heaven, and He knows that you need all these things!"

THE PRACTICE OF GODLINESS

What then must they do?

They must trust, simply and humbly, as children in the spacious home of their Father, as free from care as the lark that soars into the sky or the lily blossoming in the valley.

"*I* say to you," says Jesus, as if He wishes them to feel that *the world* teaches differently, "be not anxious for your life. Look at the birds. They do not sow or reap or gather into barns; and your heavenly Father feeds them. Surely you are of much greater value than the birds! And why be anxious about clothing? Look at the lilies! They do not work; they do not weave or spin; yet Solomon in all his glory was not clothed as beautifully as one of these. Well then, my friends, if God robes the lily of the field with such beauty, a lily that is almost hidden in the grass and that will last perhaps only a day, shall he not most surely clothe you, oh ye of little faith?"

Jesus then draws a conclusion which is contrary to all our mundane busyness: Don't be concerned about these things. Only seek the Kingdom of God first, and His righteousness, and all the rest will take care of itself; it will be thrown into your lap; He gives to His beloved as in sleep!

It is a beautiful truth, which we must not underestimate. Jesus did not warn against *over* anxiety and *great* worry. In the face of His statement we may not argue that little worries are natural and that we must be concerned about the welfare of our families or we may bring about our ruin.

Jesus' word will be of comfort to you only if you **take it as it stands.**

Live within the will of God, doing your work according to His will—not because the law demands it, nor to earn your daily bread as if your livelihood depended upon it; but for God's sake, as serving Him, always motivated by the desire to

SEEK YE FIRST

honor Him. Let your life be one continuous service of love, a service which never grows irksome, a service which will hallow even the smallest task. Seek not the external, the visible, that which the world chooses as its goal. But that which is invisible, the hidden power behind the things which we see—in short, seek the Kingdom of God, where God is enthroned and self is denied; seek all that is right, all that is in conformity with His righteousness; seek these things not only in seasons of prayer and meditation and worship, but always, in every situation, in every daily task.

Try Him, and see if His Word will not then prove true! See if He does not give you ample strength for your service of love, so that you accomplish more with less fatigue, so that you run without growing weary. See if He does not increase your joy, give abundance upon your table, and fill your heart with an exhilarating peace such as you never knew before.

Israel experienced a carefree life in the wilderness. The Lord caused water to flow from the rock, the quails to fly low, and the manna to fall upon the ground each morning. Their clothes did not wear out, nor did the soles of their shoes wear through.

Elijah enjoyed a foretaste when the angel brought him food.

The widow of Zarephath was given a few days of such blessed provision when the Lord performed a wonder upon her oil and flour.

Our Saviour demonstrated it for us when He fed the multitude by the sea of Galilee; when He made the wine at Cana; and when He bade the sea fill the net with fishes.

The day is coming when that inexpressibly glorious life will be ours in full measure, when in the mansions which He

THE PRACTICE OF GODLINESS

has prepared for us we shall find the table bounteously supplied.

If you are too concerned about the things physical, you make of these your god. Or, like the prodigal son, you are eating husks far from the house of your Father.

He who lets the Lord take care shall have a feast prepared for him.

The world has no conception of such a carefree life. They say, "If you want a thing, you must work for it."

Yet the butterfly draws sweet nectar from the flowers freely.

But the world prefers to cite the industrious ant as our example. The world chooses to live by the strength of its own hands.

Faith forgets self effort and sees only the work of God. Faith recognizes God's almighty care and our insignificant needs. Faith peers through the curtains and sees a world quite different from that which others see.

Faith that lives from the hand of God will understand the meaning of fasting. When peace of heart is disturbed, when a deep sense of unworthiness oppresses the Christian, he is like a child ashamed to take his place at father's table because he has in some way forfeited that privilege.

He whose soul is thus deeply humble before God is receptive to His grace. Never have we needed it more; and never have we been farther from the practice of fasting.

IN THE HOME

VI

In the Home

OUR purpose in this discussion of fasting is two-fold: First, to prevent others from monopolizing that which is always ours. And secondly, to lay before our people a means of edification which can be to our spiritual enrichment.

That fasting is also for us can hardly be denied. The testimony of Scripture is clear. Therefore we ought not to identify fasting with Roman Catholicism. Such a view is evidence of three errors: biased reading of the Word, ignorance of the practices of our forefathers, and lack of earnestness in the pursuit of a godly life.

Who can read the words of Jesus with unbiased mind and yet deny that Jesus placed fasting alongside of alms-giving and prayer in the godly life? He tore away the pharisaical externals, but not for a moment did He condemn fasting or make light of it.

And who, knowing the history of the church, can say that the Reformation discarded fasting with other errors? Merely the reading of *Calvin's Institutes* will convince to the contrary.

As to the earnest pursuit of a godly life—in the face of all that is written of Christian mysticism, and the witness of sincere children of God today, we cannot well close our eyes to the spiritual blessings derived from the practice of fasting.

THE PRACTICE OF GODLINESS

When we err in these three, we weaken our own position, particularly so since the Roman Catholic church holds to the truth which we are neglecting.

Moreover, has there ever been a time when Paul's lament was more true? "Whose god is the belly; of whom I tell you even weeping, that they are the enemies of the cross of Christ!"

The preparation of foods has become a fine art. Living is becoming more and more luxurious, with ever increasing demands.

In former ages there was feasting and banqueting but such luxuries were the *exception*. Simplicity was the rule.

Today, with our standards of living rising higher and higher, there are comparatively few who have not a "good" life. "Good living" has become the common ideal; men work and connive toward that goal.

Have we forgotten that supremacy of the physical impedes spiritual growth? That this catering to the desire for comforts and luxuries is detrimental to spiritual life?

What about the influence of such luxurious living upon our children?

And we ourselves are not immune!

Luxurious living is one of the chief causes of our failure to exert Christian influence.

Should we then despise fasting? What about Paul's injunction, "Bringing the flesh into subjection"?

Let the reader answer for himself, according to his own conscience.

But if personal experience gives one a right to recommend, we are constrained to witness to a hidden power there.

* * *

IN THE HOME

Though the state cannot proclaim a day of fasting and the church does not, there can nevertheless be fasting in the home, in the family.

What would this involve?

We shall not lay down rules, but merely attempt to make a few helpful suggestions, in accordance with the manner in which our forefathers observed such an occasion.

When there appears to be need of such a special day of prayer and fasting, let the father, as head of the house, prepare the family beforehand—explaining the reason for it, making clear what is the blessing desired, and instructing in true humility and confession of sin.

The day itself should begin with the gathering of the family for prayer and the reading of an appropriate portion of Scripture, in all of which the father should lead. Then all the members should be urged to private meditation and prayer, with confession of sin.

Later in the day there should be another period of united confession and prayer. And throughout the day the spirit of humble contrition should prevail in the heart and in the activities of each member of the family.

In distinction from a Thanksgiving day, which should be characterized by singing and holy joy, the day of prayer and fasting should be one of solemnity and a sorrowing for sin.

Only let us not forget Jesus' exhortation, that we fast not to be seen of men but to be "seen of Him who seeth in secret and who shall reward openly."

And may God grant that thus many of us may be led into the blessedness of richer and fuller godly living.

www.ingramcontent.com/pod-product-compliance
Lightning Source LLC
Chambersburg PA
CBHW032004080426
42735CB00007B/507